NOT MARY

NOT ROE

NOT MARY
NOT ROE

The Survival Story of a Reluctant Teen Mom

LESLIE HOPE HOLTHOFF

MERACK

NOT MARY, NOT ROE
THE SURVIVAL STORY OF A RELUCTANT TEEN MOM
BY LESLIE HOPE HOLTHOFF

Published and distributed by Merack Publishing.

Library of Congress Control Number: 2022911773
Holthoff, Leslie Hope
Not Mary, Not Roe: The Survival Story of a Reluctant Teen Mom
ISBN Paperback 978-1-957048-59-8
ISBN Hardcover 978-1-957048-61-1
ISBN eBook 978-1-957048-60-4

DEDICATION

I'd like to dedicate this book to the three Jameses in my life:

To my father. Thank you for always seeing my potential and not just the person in front of you. Thank you for forgiving me for so many mistakes and loving me through every one of them. Thank you for always having my back, always making me laugh, and seeing this world through the same lens as me.

To Tyler. Without you my story wouldn't be worthy of these pages. You've been my biggest challenge, the biggest catalyst to my success, and the one person who seems to have never questioned what I am capable of. Thank you. I hope one day you realize that what you are looking for is already inside you.

To Hatteras. I see in you a lifetime of amazing things. I see the same drive, the same potential, and that same burning desire that I have felt boiling over inside of me since I was just a kid. You are an exceptional human and I am so proud to be partially responsible for your existence. I can't wait to watch you make this life yours.

CONTENTS

INTRODUCTION

In America, teen pregnancy has been on a steady decline since the early nineties. As of 2020, the teen birth rate for girls ages 15-19 was 15 per 1,000 females, according to the U.S. Centers for Disease Control and Prevention. For the 15-17 age group, the number dropped to 38,587. Below the age of 15, 1,765 girls gave birth in 2020. In 1993, when I got pregnant at the age of 15 there were 190,535 births to mothers 15-17 and 12,554 to girls younger than 15.

In 1993 I was one of 3,621 teenage girls in Virginia who was pregnant. A pregnant teenage girl today would be one of only 804. While these statistics are encouraging, there are still girls who are raising children before they themselves have reached adulthood. Less than two percent of girls who give birth as a teenager will go on to earn a college degree by age 30. Fifty percent of them won't make it to high school graduation.

I was lucky enough to graduate on time from high school but I did not achieve a college degree by 30. I was 33 when I earned my Bachelor's degree and 35 when I earned my Master's. By then, my son, born to me when I was 16, was already older than I was when I had him.

I didn't know any of these statistics when I found out that I was pregnant in the fall of 1993. I didn't know of any other girls who had gotten pregnant. I didn't know any other girls who had given birth. In the nineties, MTV was at the height of its cultural influence but the network's Teen Mom series wasn't on the lineup until 2009. I had been told women didn't have children until they were married and, as I understood it, it wasn't even a choice— that was just the way it was. In other words, I didn't imagine it was possible to be pregnant before marriage.

The big tragedy, if one chooses to see it that way, happened when I was fifteen. My pregnancy was the culmination of 15 years of having my voice ignored by various boys and men. Some of my male friends and cousins laughed as I screamed "no" and "stop" while they wrestled and tackled me. There was the boy on the bus when I was ten who thought he had the right to feel my body as I walked down the aisle. There were the boys I dated as I got older who always seemed to want to go further than I wanted to go, and "no" or "I don't want to" just meant they would try harder. By the time I stood staring at the two pink lines on a pregnancy test, my life already felt like it belonged to someone else. It reinforced my feeling, once again, that what I wanted didn't matter. People who knew me (and strangers, too) asked, "Why couldn't she just say no?"—as if I hadn't said it.

When I was 17, I had an encounter with a boy I thought I loved. It was after I gave birth to my son. We were being intimate but I was very clear that I could not, would not, have sex. I was not on birth control, because, quite frankly, I didn't want to ever have sex again after what I had been through. I trusted this boy and thought that I was safe. But I was not safe. As time went on, he decided that my words didn't matter, that me being mostly naked was consent enough, and he had sex with me anyway. I was devastated, and scared, and I felt incredibly alone. The word rape danced around in my mind but that word didn't seem to fit. I loved this person and I thought that he loved me. I put myself in a situation that I thought was safe and I was wrong. I voluntarily took things to a point, thinking it was okay to call the shots, but once again I was faced with the fact that my words were not enough to protect my body.

Having already had one baby, I was paranoid that I was going to be pregnant again. In the days leading up to my eventual period, I had to make what I was convinced was a life or death choice. I decided that there was absolutely no way I would bring another child into this world. I decided that I would have an abortion, in a medical clinic or with a coat hanger in my bathroom, whatever it took to make this version of me go away. Being pregnant was the worst thing I could imagine. I was willing to sacrifice everything—my life, if necessary—to keep from bearing that shame, that burden, again.

I couldn't wait to turn 18, leave my parents house, and embark on my own journey where I would be able to make decisions for myself. I thought becoming an adult would open a magical door that I could walk through on my birthday and on the other side I would find that suddenly my voice had changed and people would care what I wanted for the first time in my life.

And so I embarked on my adult life determined to ease the burden I had placed on myself and the people I loved. I wanted more than anything to find a way to fit in somewhere, to find my place in a world that I was told wasn't meant for a teen mom. I hadn't followed the rules and so I became a misfit. I was still a child in so many ways, yet I had to behave like an adult because I was a mother. I hadn't been old enough to marry without my parents' consent, to vote, to buy beer, to get divorced, to not go to high school, but I was old enough to bring another human into this world and be made to take care of it.

What a shame that I had been taught that abortion was murder and therefore not a real option for me. What a shame that the baby inside of me was more important than me, than my childhood. What a shame that I thought that having the baby was "the right thing to do," and that someone, *anyone*, would be there to help me. What a shame. Because we lost. As a society, we all lost.

I was an awful mother to my son. He deserved better. Having a child at 16 left scars—in the physical sense, of course, but in less obvious ways as well. It would take me over a decade to become comfortable with sex and not view it as something that men wanted and took from me. I had only ever been taught that as a girl, as a woman, I wasn't supposed to want it, and I was always to say no. If I ever admitted to having sexual desire, or my own wants and needs, I was a whore. But there are no whores. There are just women. Regular, human women behaving in perfectly normal human ways.

We can't teach our girls that sex is something men desire and steal from us. We can't teach our girls that if they have sex before marriage, if someone talks them into it, they have been outsmarted. We can't teach our girls to say "no" for decades and then expect them to get married and suddenly be able to articulate their wants and needs. We can't decide to *not* teach our children what sex is, that it's some secret that will remain hidden until they walk down the aisle. We can't take away their knowledge of what sex is, and then force them to bear the consequences. Knowledge is power. Ignorance is not bliss. It sets girls up for failure.

I was no Virgin Mary, but I was so young and naive I thought I might as well have been. I was no "Jane Roe" who could fight for what she knew she wanted. Norma McCorvey was a decade older than I was when she became the face of the historic 1973 Supreme Court decision. I was a little girl. A girl so full of potential I can't imagine what she could have brought to the world if given the opportunity to be something other than a teen mother.

Not every mother is full of joy when they place that bundle in her arms. I wasn't. I know that my son may be thankful to be alive, but he struggles, too. He has to live with the trauma of being raised by a mother who didn't want to be a mother. By a mother who was always broke, always scared, and almost always sad—at least for the first ten years of his life.

We can do better. I taught my boys that we accept everyone for where they are and who they are. I taught them to love and care about others. I chose to teach them about sex in a way that will hopefully keep them safe and in control, as much as that's possible, of their own lives. I taught them to honor the wishes of women and not to push girls into sex. I was never tempted to utter the words that they were supposed to wait until marriage and that if they didn't they would go to hell. I have tried to build a relationship with them that is open and honest communication about sex so that I can be a source of true information, an outlet other than the internet.

I ask that you read this book with an open mind. So many people who were incredibly important to my survival didn't make it into the book, and those that did certainly didn't get enough of the credit they deserve. I have shared a lot in this book, including some of my deepest and darkest moments—much of it for the first time. Even those who love me and to whom I am closest haven't heard the whole story.

Most importantly, I hope that you read this and understand that there is no across-the-board "right" answer to life. I was lucky enough to have parents who loved me despite my mistakes and made sure I was always okay. So many girls don't have that support. So many girls are like I was, too young and too naive to even be able to understand what is happening. I beg you to forgive them. I beg you not to raise judgment. I beg you to choose your words wisely and to remember that you don't know her story.

The worst, most awful thing that happened to me actually became the thing that makes me uniquely qualified for my job as a divorce and coparenting coach. I have been a young, single mother and I have been a married mother. I have given my child my own last name and that of my husband. I have raised a child with a stepparent, I have co-parented with two different teams for almost 30 years. My children have two different fathers and so I have two entirely different stories related to parenting a child with another adult. It's not the way I would have written my story but it is still mine. My story has helped me guide fathers to better understand their daughters, communicate better with their exes, and co-parent at a level that they are proud of. As a coach, I use what I have learned to benefit others.

In an effort to help the children who have children, and their choice not to, I have created the The Holthoff March Project, a non-profit which focuses on supporting a womens right to choose, sex education for all, and offering support to help those who choose to become young parents find success through education and home ownership. If you would like to know more or to offer support please visit www.theHolthoffMarchProject.org.

CHAPTER ONE

In any society, there are certain social norms. Norms are not laws; a person cannot be tried in court for violating them. Instead, they are a set of beliefs designed to guide us and to keep order. Breaking a social norm may not land us in jail but it most certainly can isolate us from our friends and family.

I was taught all of the "right" social norms growing up. Why were they "right"? Because my parents said so. Because every adult I knew said so. Because the world was divided into "us" and "them" and you did *not* want to be "them". "Them" was anyone not like us. Anyone who was a different color, different class, anyone who was addicted, tattooed, or maybe even just someone who dyed their hair an unnatural shade. "We" were "good" people. Our social norms were very traditionally split for men and women and it would take me the better part of twenty years to understand the implications of that.

It was the 1980s. We went to church on Sunday. My father worked hard and my mother raised us girls. We didn't drink too much (usually) and we certainly didn't do drugs. We didn't fight and we didn't go to jail. We married one time, the love of our lives, of course, and we stayed married until one of us died. During weekends and holidays the women cooked large meals and made plates for their kids and husbands, and, when everyone was done, they also cleaned up. The men—as a reward for working all week, I perceived—got to hang out and drink beer. They talked about projects and politics and football and laughed a lot. The way I saw it, the men worked and the women didn't. It would take a long time for me to see that the women were working, too, and to view the household as a division of labor.

The first church I remember was the Church of St. Therese, a Catholic church near our home in Chesapeake, Virginia that stood tall with a huge, open-armed, St. Therese hanging at the front. The chapel felt huge and the echo made it feel even bigger. The pews were wooden and uncomfortable and staying quiet was hard for me. Nevertheless, my entire extended family went there every Sunday. It was the church where my parents got married and where my sisters and I were baptized. When my paternal grandfather passed we held his funeral there on Christmas Eve. I know now that my grandfather had been very sick but back then my family never told children anything scary or sad and so when he died it felt like it came out of nowhere. The surprise made me feel as if my parents could die at any moment. It was terrifying.

On Sundays, my mother had the responsibility of wrangling all three of us girls and had to push my dad along as well. Getting out of the house on time always seemed stressful and challenging. My parents loved to have fun and Saturday nights were spent with their friends and, when we were lucky, ended in big sleepovers with kids piled everywhere. Dad believed strongly in going to church but even he didn't like those early Sunday mornings.

On weekdays, my father left for work at an ungodly hour before the sun came up. My mother got up with him each day to make his breakfast and pack his lunch. I used to try every day to wake up and get a chance to see him before he left even though I would be admonished for being awake so early.

When he arrived home at the end of the day, it was much the same; my mother prepared dinner and the table for her family. What should have been quality family time was usually ruined by me, because I was always getting in trouble for not eating my dinner. I was the pickiest eater on Earth. I rarely wanted what she made and so I played with my food and exasperated my mother further. For added fun, I would change what I would and would not eat, frequently. Sometimes noodles were in, sometimes noodles were out. The only two things that were always on the list were pizza and hot dogs. I ate hot dogs any way they could be served. I feel confident that I have eaten more hot dogs than any other human.

The gender roles I learned as a child were stereotypical of the eighties. I could see them at play in my own home, my grandparents' home, and in all my aunts' and uncles' houses. I had a few friends as I got older whose mothers worked outside the home, but that was still pretty uncommon back then, and none of them seemed to have jobs that interested me—they were grocery store clerks or teachers or nurses. But I loved paperwork, and in my imagination I would work in a bank. In our middle-class neighborhood, us kids felt safe with our moms at home, our dads at work, and our bikes taking us anywhere our legs could pedal—as long as we promised to be home before the streetlights came on.

I begged my dad to let me help him on whatever project he was working on in our garage. I never felt more special than I did when the two of us went off by ourselves. I painted the mailbox, learned to shoot a rifle and a bow—and how not to be afraid of green snakes. My dad and I collected locust shells and watched the stars through his telescope. He took me to the submarine launches at the shipyard, to boat shows in Virginia Beach, and he once even bought me a Swatch Watch—perhaps the most iconic brand of watch in the eighties. It was colorful and had a face protector that could be swapped out and customized. My dad made me feel like the most important person in the world.

My grandfather Lenny, my mom's dad, was another man I was drawn to. Whenever we visited him and my four uncles, there would be football watching (only the Washington Redskins), beer drinking, and a "man" project. Once, when I was six, my grandfather decided to put in a pool and asked all four of his sons and his son-in-law to dig the hole. I wanted to help, too, but it was so hot outside. All the men were shirtless. I was jealous.

"Why can't I take off my shirt?" I asked.

My grandfather laughed and told me I could. I ripped that thing off like it was strangling me. Lenny and my uncles thought this was hilarious: a little girl, shirtless, trying to help grown men dig a hole. After a few minutes, I realized they were laughing *at* me and I was filled with embarrassment. I put my shirt on and headed back inside with the women.

When we visited Lenny, my cousins were often around as well. My cousin David was only slightly younger than me. David loved to tackle me and wrestle—unbothered by my screaming, fighting him off, and crying. My grandfather and uncles thought watching us "wrestle" was the most hilarious thing they had ever seen. I'm not sure if they were more impressed with David's skills (he later became a wrestling champion) or if they just found boys beating up girls funny. I don't think they realized that this is how girls learn that their bodies are not their own.

The year my youngest sister Meghan was born, my father, who had been working tirelessly at his company, was told that he could not move up any further because he didn't have a college degree. When he told us the news I could feel the anger vibrating off his body. He thought it was completely ridiculous that someone else could be promoted over him, not because of skill in the field or on-the-job success, but because of a classroom. It had never occurred to me that a college degree was a requirement for being successful. No one in my family had been to college. It seemed frivolous. Since my father had been able to out-earn all his counterparts without a degree, I wondered why anyone would waste their time and money with college unless their goal was to be a doctor or a lawyer. When I was growing up, my parents certainly didn't push me to go to college—though I don't know if that was because I was a girl or because they genuinely didn't see the purpose in it for anyone. This would become a source of contempt as the years progressed, and one of the biggest barriers I would have to overcome.

After being told he couldn't move any higher in the company my father decided to take things into his own hands. He partnered with someone he had met through his business dealings and together they decided to create their own business. Dad's partner would provide the money and Dad would be responsible for doing the work. They found an opportunity to do general construction for a local shipyard using Dad's two best assets: carpentry and math. This act of defiance, ingenuity, and grit — my father's refusal to let one "no" get in his way—stuck with me perhaps more than anything else I learned in my childhood. His entire career was built on solving problems people thought there was no answer to, and he found solace in finding a way around any roadblock he encountered.

Before his success as an entrepreneur, my dad was just a man with a newborn, a special-needs daughter, and me, plus a stay-at-home wife. I can't imagine how angry, or how desperate, or how motivated he must have been to have decided to start this company just two months after my sister was born. I can only imagine the look on my mother's face as he told her his plans. My mother had given up her career as an X-ray technician when she had me, so my father was the sole provider for the family while my mother concentrated on raising us girls and running a household.

My father's first act at his new business was to bring on an employee, my mother's littlest brother, Mike. When I was born, Mike was only twenty. He absolutely adored me. He would pick me up every Sunday, when I got old enough, and take me to Chuck E. Cheese or to the local park where we would feed the ducks and ride the toy train. Somehow, he decided my nickname should be Doodoo and that's what he called me. I, not quite in my creative element yet, decided his nickname would be Uncle Doodoo. It stuck.

My dad and my Uncle Doodoo got to work. The story goes that when they started they had nothing to sit on but five-gallon buckets. But over time, their business grew. Before long they had a full-time secretary, an actual office, and the list of employees increased.

My dad was an exceptional carpenter. He made us highchairs with beautiful inscriptions and designs, rocking horses, and lots of other things. To this day, those gifts are worth more to me than any amount of money. To see the bassinet my dad made when I was born with my name and birthday inscribed melts a place in my heart.

My parents made sacrifices. I remember begging my mother for a Cabbage Patch Kid one Christmas. Cabbage Patch Kids were the be-all of dolls in the 80s. On Christmas morning, I received a homemade doll my mother had made with pantyhose as part of her face. I complained that it didn't have a hard face like a *real* Cabbage Patch Kid.

The next year I made the same request to Santa. This time I got a handmade doll with a hard face. It was better, and I was happy, but it didn't have Xavier's signature on its rear end. But the third year, when my dad's business was doing well, I finally received my dream come true! A real Cabbage Patch Kid.

It was around this same time that my mother, the professional housewife, struck out for some independence. Women everywhere were beginning to throw Tupperware parties and launch direct marketing campaigns with companies like Avon and Mary Kay. My mother and a friend of hers began making wood figures that they painted. They would make bears, houses, pretty much anything they fancied. My dad supplied the wood and taught my mom how to use the bandsaw to create exactly what she wanted. Her creations ranged in size from just inches to about a foot tall. Their other friends began to notice and soon they were hosting their own craft parties.

My mom had to fit in time for herself when she could, usually during our nap times or after we were in bed. She often had to make arrangements with my dad or find babysitters to watch us while she went to her craft parties. Even now, I get the feeling my father was annoyed that he was having to babysit and change his schedule for something he deemed not worth it. He was never the type of husband to tell my mother what she could and could not do—after all, he *did* teach her how to use the bandsaw and help her create products—but that didn't mean he wasn't annoyed with the responsibility of child care.

At the time, from my seven-year-old viewpoint, I felt angry at my mother for finding something else to do with her time. In my eyes, she didn't "need" to do these things to make money—I saw it as a hobby that took her away from my sisters and me. But in hindsight, I am so proud of her badassery. It was pretty ambitious for a woman with three kids under the age of eight, one of whom had special needs, to have a wood crafting business.

Most of what I believed—or had been led to believe—about life and how it "should" go was established during these years, when I was a kid. The church taught us that two people, a man and a woman, fell in love, got married, and later had children. Men worked. Women raised children, kept the home clean, and prepared meals.

CHAPTER TWO

As the eighties came to an end, a lot changed for us. My parents decided to move to a new town and began building a new house. This meant my father was even more absent than before, and it also meant I had to go to a new school for fifth grade. Moving to a rural town was hard. It was a culture shock, for one. I hadn't known any Black people in our neighborhood before now, and in my previous school there were only a few Black or mixed children. My first teacher in the new school was Black and I was one of only a handful of white students. In fact, in my new school, I was the minority. While my parents didn't speak of race much, my grandfather Lenny did—and loudly. The son of Irish immigrants, he had very distinct beliefs about the difference between white and Black people. To him, Black people were not people.

He truly saw anyone who he considered non-white as a completely separate race—and that race was not human.

The weight of this prejudice hung on me like a cloak. Up until this point I hadn't known any Black people myself, so I had no reason to doubt what my grandfather said or even give any of it much thought. But now I was surrounded by Black people—they were not only my peers but also leaders at the school. And I liked my teacher, Ms. Day. I couldn't make sense of how the things my grandfather said could be true if I had a Black teacher and Black friends. My grandfather's hate was a huge source of internal conflict that took me years to understand and come to terms with.

I hated my new school and I hated the bus even more. Every day I rode the bus home. Every day I sat down and waited patiently for my stop, when I would have to walk down the long aisle to the bus door. Every day as I walked past, one boy would reach his hand out and rub it all over my butt. I was ten years old and had never been touched by anyone other than my parents before. I was mortified. I wish I could say I punched him but the truth is, I froze. It happened so often, even when I managed to say "stop," it wasn't enough. I took to wearing my backpack lower and lower, trying to get it to block my butt so he would leave me alone. It was about a quarter mile from the bus stop to our new house and I spent most of the walk crying. This went on for months until finally my mother, becoming more and more concerned about the dried tears on my face, finally convinced me to tell her what was wrong.

I have no idea what my mom said to that school, or what that school said to that boy, but I was never touched again on that bus. Still, that was just a new person, in a new environment, where my words were ignored. It was added to the list of times I was forced to allow someone to do something to my body I didn't want. I didn't want him to touch me but I didn't know how to make him stop. That he felt so entitled to do something so personal, invasive, and sexual to someone else who clearly didn't want it stunned me. It made me feel helpless, worthless, and not in control of my body.

In my new classroom, I was terrified. I knew absolutely no one and the kids liked picking on me. I guess I looked like an easy target. The girl who sat directly behind me said mean things to me all day long. She would laugh at my long blonde hair, she would laugh at what I wore, she picked on me in any way she could.

One day our teacher gave us an assignment to bring in a picture of our house. I proudly brought in a picture of the new house my father had built. Once that girl saw the size of my house, she changed her tune.

The house my father had spent the last year building was on the banks of Jones Creek. The creek gave the property deep water access to the James River and the first thing he built—even before the house—was a large pier with several boat lifts and a floating dock. Jones Creek was wide, with a marsh on each side that made it look even wider. It was a hot spot for water skiing or tubing, with plenty of room for boats to turn around.

The second thing Dad built was a detached garage that housed all of his tools and projects. It was his new favorite place. Finally, he designed and built his dream house. It was two stories, 5,000 square feet, with white vinyl siding, dormer windows, and a three-car garage. The house was pretty magnificent.

Suddenly, the girl in my class acted as though we were best friends. It was confusing that my biggest enemy had suddenly become my best friend. I was struggling to fit in at this new school or understand these mean girls. I was also beginning to be treated differently because of the perception my parents had money.

The one good thing that happened to me that year was meeting Erin, who would become a lifelong friend. I was in line behind her at the water fountain one day, and when it was my turn, she spun around and sprayed water at my face. At the time, I had a haircut that looked like a water spout. The hallway erupted with laughter and even though she was making fun of me, I had to admit it was funny. Erin's mother was a teacher at the high school and her father was the fire chief, so she knew everyone in town and everyone knew her. She was the first person I knew with divorced parents; the first person I knew that spent weekends somewhere different from where she spent her weeks. She was one of the first people that forced me to begin questioning what I had been taught about divorce. Her parents were both great and treated me like family. I felt so at home in her home(s), and it came as a shock to me since I had been taught that only bad people got divorced.

In our new small town, eighth grade was the start of high school. So, at 13, I was placed in a school filled with teenagers much older and much further on their journey through puberty than I was. I weighed about 90 pounds and had long hair down to my waist with pink-framed glasses that took up half my face. By some twist of fate I found my way to the junior varsity cheerleading squad, which afforded me a new group of friends as well as a sense of belonging. The feelings of camaraderie were short lived, however, as I hated exercise, sweat, and almost everyone. I was really great to be around.

Despite the fact that fitting in was my number one goal, I was totally unequipped to fit in with anyone. I was lazy, bored and always very tired. I would never have left my bed if my parents had allowed it. My lack of motivation drove me to do what most girls in my position would do: I faked injuries. A lot of injuries. At the ripe old age of 13 I complained about my knees, my back, my legs, my toes… the list goes on. You name it, mine hurt.

We had cheer practice every day after school (which to me, of course, felt excessive) so, naturally, I kept a full arsenal of excuses. I had perpetual hip problems. The captain of the cheerleading squad was a girl named Gia. Gia was a year older than me and she was stunningly beautiful, though she had absolutely no idea. She was tall, five-foot ten, with perfect olive skin, dark eyes, and dark hair—like a modern-day Pocahontas. She seemed like someone who was destined to escape our small town and embrace all the world outside had to offer. She knew she held power over everyone and that she was the leader, but she didn't think she deserved it. Still, being on her good side was a necessary part of making it in high school. Gia and I were friends—until one day we weren't. It was raining. On rainy days we were forced to practice in the cafeteria where we were joined by the soccer team running laps around the room. On this particular day our team was working on a pyramid. Of course, I was having some sort of "issue" with my pre-pubescent hips. But I didn't want to miss practice altogether (did I mention the soccer team?) so I sat on the bleachers to offer my "emotional support" to the team.

I thought the situation was conducive to my suggestions, corrections, and general good coaching.

I read the room wrong.

It turns out people doing the hard work don't want advice from old ladies sitting on the sidelines. Gia, a base in our pyramid due to her height and strength, quickly sat down the girl standing on her shoulder and without warning quickly began kicking my ass.

As she approached me the room stopped. The soccer team slowed their running, the other cheerleaders froze where they had landed, and I was completely unprepared for what was about to happen next. Was she going to tell me a secret? Drink some of my water? At the last minute, out of reflex I suppose, I was able to put my hands in front of my face and block the first blow, which then landed directly on the top of my head. It was soon followed by more fists to the head. I should have been faster, realized what was coming and had a few seconds to prepare.

I should have had time to run, or hit, or *anything*. But I didn't, I barely had time to cover my face. So I sat there, hands trying to block the oncoming blows until finally she was pulled off of me. Gia got plenty of good hits in and then my hips didn't hurt so bad. My head, neck, and shoulders took the brunt of the beating, but my ego got it the worst.

Since it was my lucky day the soccer teams (yes, JV *and* Varsity were both there) ran over to get into the action. Thank god they didn't have cell phones.

Looking back now, I wonder if perhaps I wasn't a great teammate. It turns out that when you have "sore hips" and are regularly sitting out of practice, those who are actually practicing have no interest in your critiques. Lesson learned.

After that, I begged my parents to let me go to a different school. But I wouldn't tell them what had happened, so, back to school I went. I was upset by the fact that they had the money to send me to private school but they wouldn't. Maybe if given all the facts they would have made a different decision, but I just couldn't bear to tell them.

But it wasn't all bad that year, either. I met Paul at a football game. He said "hi" and I said "hello", which he thought was hilarious. He claims to have fallen in love with me the moment he set eyes on me. He worked weekends at his grandfather's cabinet shop, which I found very impressive. As an incoming eighth grader in a high school full of older teenagers, I thought it was a big deal that a boy in tenth grade was paying attention to me. I'd never had a serious boyfriend before, and this felt like it could be the real thing. I felt flattered and a little taken aback by how positive he was that we were meant to be together.

He was hopelessly devoted to me, which was great at first. Then I felt smothered. When we broke up I did my best to avoid him. If he saw me talking to someone else or heard I was dating someone else, he would start fights or punch things certain to break his hand.

Matters were complicated by the fact that I had a major crush on someone else. Justin was my first true love. After I saw him skateboard into the community pool the summer before eighth grade, I was smitten. I just knew he was the one for me. I felt about him the way Paul felt about me. He and Paul were in the same grade but he was about six months older, making him almost two and a half years older than me. He was a small guy. He kept his dark hair shaved, but just long enough that it felt cool to run your hands through it. He was always dressed in the most fashionable brand names and was the type to start trends with the clothes he wore and how he wore them. He drove a Suzuki Samurai, the epitome of cool. I couldn't get enough. I was head over heels.

Justin's friend Andre set us up over the phone. With the phone cord stretched as long as it would go, I hid in my closet, trying to get some privacy. When Valentine's Day came on the horizon, Justin started talking about what he was going to get me as a gift.

He gave me a new clue each day.

"It's long and hard."

"You use it to get in somewhere warm and dark."

"It makes you feel good."

"You could use it daily, even more than once a day."

"The place it goes to is pink."

"It gets wet."

For me, at 13, this was torture. I wasn't even sure I knew what he was implying. I thought he was probably talking about sex, but I didn't know for certain. I had been very sheltered and even the movies I had seen up to that point were rated PG. I guessed he wanted to have sex with me, but I couldn't even stomach the idea. Even the idea of a penis was off-putting, terrifying. But I liked Justin so much I was nervous to turn him down. It took all the courage I had to tell him I didn't think I could accept his "gift." Justin laughed and kept on with his hints, making the situation much worse and continuing to torment me.

When Valentine's Day finally arrived, he came over to bring me my gift.

It was a toothbrush.

He laughed so hard. I didn't think it was funny at all. He had made me feel stupid. I felt he had purposely tried to trick me and make me feel dumb. And, as if that wasn't bad enough, I got a toothbrush for Valentine's Day.

I didn't yet understand what it meant that a person who claimed to care about me would go so far out of his way to humiliate me, belittle me, and purposely cause me stress. I had heard rumors that Justin's home life was "different." Justin and his brothers cussed openly to their parents. Once I witnessed it with my own eyes when I was at his house with some friends. Justin's mother came into his room to check on us.

"What are you doing in here?" Justin hissed. "Get the fuck out and go make me a sandwich."

This was shocking to me. Since his parents were married and lived in a nice neighborhood, I assumed they were like "us." That could not have been farther from the truth.

————————

That same year, a new girl walked right into school with her matching skirt set and her hair half up and half down.

She was about to change the dynamic between Erin and me, adding our missing third. She was shorter than me, about 5'3" and very pretty, the kind of pretty you noticed from the other side of the room. She had dirty blonde hair and really pretty green eyes. But that's not what struck me most about her. It was the air of confidence she was carrying as she walked into the commons area. We were 13. Nobody had confidence like that. But Kelly did.

Once we met, we were fast friends. We were in some of the same classes and she joined the cheering squad with Erin and me. I would go to her house and she would come to mine, and what I remember most is laughter. We laughed a lot. At first, anyway.

Kelly was the kind of girl who did whatever she wanted. She always knew exactly what she wanted and she would find a way to get it, no matter who got hurt in the process. She didn't quite know how to tell the truth, especially to her parents. Before we would do anything, her mother would say, "Make wise decisions!"

We rarely did.

But from the beginning of our friendship, Kelly and I had a problem: We had the same taste in boys. Justin and Paul kept things interesting between us. It felt like at every point in high school, one of us was dating one of them. And it changed several times. I was more in love with Justin, and she was more in love with Paul. But Paul was more in love with me and Justin was more in love with himself. It was way worse than a love triangle. A love wrecktangle?

Soon, there was more drama than laughter.

In spite of the warning signs, I was in *love* with Justin. Love, love, love. I wrote poetry. I dreamt about him. I fantasized about our life together. I wanted nothing more than to be Mrs. Justin. My day revolved around getting to see him at school or passing him in the hallways. When he spoke to me I was in heaven.

Sex was everywhere in high school. It felt like everyone was having it and I was the exception for not. I made it all the way through my ninth-grade year without losing my virginity, which felt like an accomplishment. I said no so many times it was starting to feel like all I could say. In fact, I was the last one in our friend group to do it, and I felt like the last one in school.

It happened the summer after ninth grade. I was at a pool party, and I left with Justin. His parents were gone so we went to his house. It only happened once and I was so filled with shame and regret I wanted to throw up. I didn't understand how so many of my friends were doing this on a regular basis. I hated it. And I hated myself. It was a terrible experience. I don't know how, but I worked up the nerve to tell Justin it was never going to happen again.

Not long after, Justin came to school with hickies on his neck. When I confronted him, he ended it with me. He told me that he didn't want to hurt Becky, the girl he had hooked up with and cheated on me with. For the sake of her feelings, he thought we should break up. I was heartbroken. I couldn't imagine ever loving again. I spent countless days lying on the floor of my bedroom weeping, listening to Reba McIntire, and drowning my sorrow in depressing songs.

When Justin and I broke up, Paul came to pick up the pieces. We decided to start dating again, but he was so depressed. Paul talked constantly about how he knew we were going to break up. He was mourning the loss before it occurred. Looking back, I wish I had understood then that he needed help. But I was fifteen and still wrapped up in everything that had happened with Justin.

One night while I was sleeping over at a friend's house we went to Paul's apartment. His mother was working out of town so it was all his. I remember a bottle of Boone's Farm Strawberry Hill wine. I remember how the apartment didn't have any furniture and how the carpet felt on my back. I remember that Paul was wearing a necklace that reminded me of one my grandfather wore and for some reason that made me feel safe. I just kept feeling like I was supposed to want to have sex, but I didn't. Paul loved me, of that I was sure. My body was trembling, my legs shaking uncontrollably. I don't really know how my pants came off but my shirt stayed in place covering what part of my body it could.

Immediately upon him entering me I started to cry and he stopped. He attempted to comfort me and hugged me and said he was sorry. But it was too late. I had allowed myself to go where I swore I wouldn't. The shame and self-hatred were overwhelming. I went into the bathroom and took a shower with the water as hot as it would go, burning the sin from my body. I wept uncontrollably. Having only ever been taught that sex was something married people did, I am not sure I had any comprehension what things led to sex, what to expect, or how to talk about it. My tools for stopping it or slowing it down didn't exist. After many many tears, my friend and I returned to her home, where I curled up in her bed in the fetal position and spent the night trying to sleep and forget what had just happened.

I didn't know it yet, but Paul and I had just changed the entire trajectory of our lives.

The next year would be the hardest year of my life. I took the pregnancy test after school one day at Kelly's house. When the two pink lines appeared, I wept in her arms, and her mother's arms, too. Her mother drove me to my house and told my mom while I sat in the car.

I was too scared, embarrassed, and ashamed to be there when my mother heard the news. From my vantage point in the car I watched as my father crossed from the shed up the stairs to the front door where just inside my mother was crying and begging Kelly's mother to say it wasn't true.

But it was true. My parents moved into the formal living room, where we never went, and I joined them there. Or at least some part of me did. When I opened the front door to go inside, pausing momentarily, something—or someone—else took over. It felt as if I floated into that living room to meet them. The me I had known just hours ago was dead and this new girl, this new life, was frozen in time. My legs had become attached to the floor and were unable to move, so something carried me forward.

My father paced, angry. He said some pretty awful things, most of which I know he didn't mean, but it broke me nonetheless. My mother wept, barely able to catch her breath in between sobs. How could I have done this to them?

I am not sure my parents could have been more surprised if I told them I had grown a penis and baby testicles. I fully expected them to kick me out. I imagined moving into a shelter. I had no idea what was going to happen next. The truth is, I barely knew anything. I barely knew how babies came. I barely knew how men came. I had only recently learned that you didn't *have* to wait until marriage. Everything I knew about the possibility of having a baby out of wedlock was based solely on the song *Papa Don't Preach* by Madonna.

> *"The one you warned me all about*
> *The one you said I could do without*
> *We're in an awful mess*
> *and I don't mean maybe, please*
> *Papa don't preach I'm in trouble deep*
> *Papa don't preach, I've been losing sleep*
> *But I made up my mind, I'm keeping my baby."*

That's it. That's all I knew.

I lied and told them both it had been my first time. That it was my second seemed irrelevant and hurtful. My dad wanted Paul and me to get married. I told him I knew I had made a mistake but marrying Paul would have been another. I told him I wouldn't do it.

My religious upbringing had led me to believe that this was God's doing, that He wanted me to bear this cross.

I felt obligated to do so. No matter how badly I did not want the child growing inside me I thought it had to be happening to me for a reason—a reason too big for my little mind to comprehend. God had chosen Mary, right? She also had a baby out of wedlock. I had been taught that God created babies from the moment of conception and at the time I had no reason to question that.

My father believed I was going to hell. His Catholic upbringing went against everything standing in front of him that he loved so much. He thought my life was over.

In a sense, it was.

The day I took that pregnancy test and told my parents I was pregnant was the worst day of my entire life. No lie can hide a pregnant belly. No amount of praying can make you unpregnant. No age is old enough to comprehend the task that motherhood lays before you. There was no way to un-do what had been done and it mattered not if I understood it. Quite frankly I ceased to exist as a person that day and the barely formed life inside of me started to get to call the shots. Life as I had known it for fifteen years was over and in this new life I was obligated to live for this child.

———————————

I was depressed, lost, torn, and completely broken. I did not want to have a baby. I did not want the world to know what I had done. And so, I wrote about it in the journal I was required to keep in English class. That journal was a place to unleash my soul and try to make sense out of the hell I felt I had created. Each day I folded the paper in half (the teacher said doing so would keep her from reading it), scared that if she read it she would have me committed, even though that would have been an escape.

Then one day my journal went missing. I'll never forget the tears in the eyes of my teacher when she told me it was gone. She was so upset. Nothing like that had ever happened in her classroom before, she said. I was in shock. I didn't understand how she could have misplaced something so important, so personal. But I soon found out it wasn't her fault. Kelly got a boy in the class to steal it for her. She ripped out the pages and passed them around the cafeteria for everyone to read.

I already felt like the biggest freak in the world, like someone who could not be more alone. Then, the cafeteria erupted with pointed fingers and laughter.

Having the words that I wrote in private thrown out into the world changed me. I have never quite been able to write as freely as I did back then. I was always scared that whatever I said would be read by unapproved eyes and used against me.

After that night at his apartment, Paul and I quickly broke up. I couldn't stand to see him or talk to him as it instantly took me back to that horrendous night. His depression and guilt about what had happened were more than our teenage relationship could take.

Then, of course, Justin started talking to me again. We were "talking" when I found out I was pregnant. He begged me to abort. Everything I knew about abortion was Christian-based pro-life propaganda. Abortion was murder, I had been taught to believe. So even though legally it was an option, it wasn't an option for me. I didn't think paying for one sin with another made sense. When I told Justin I wasn't having an abortion, he told me that dating me ever again would be too shameful for his family and he stopped talking to me. I was broken-hearted all over again. I picked the child inside me over everyone else and in turn lost the man I thought was the love of my life.

I seriously thought I would never love again. I thought that choosing to have my child literally meant no one would ever love me romantically.

I was a scared little girl with no concept of what was happening to my body. I had only recently begun to grow breasts and begun turning from a girl into a woman. I spent countless hours in the school library looking up pregnancy in the encyclopedias, trying to learn what I could in an attempt to feel less clueless about what was happening. I felt like I had been thrown into a secret world that had been kept from me my entire life. Having never had a single conversation about sex or been taught the consequences associated with it, I was pregnant. I had been taught only that sex was something married people did—I barely understood that it was even a choice, something people *chose* to do. Health class at school was of no help—we never learned about sex at all, only anatomy.

My mother decided we needed to go to an actual OBGYN to confirm that I was indeed pregnant. She brought me to her doctor, a 70-year-old man. I was taken into a brightly-lit room which was filled with several nurses and my mother. I whimpered the entire time. It felt like I was being violated and raped. I was mortified being sprawled out on the table. Having my mother there made it worse, even more embarrassing. I know she was being as supportive as she could be, but the exam itself was humiliating. It was my first time at the gynecologist. I didn't know having five people in the room was strange, or that I had any say in the matter.

When the exam was finally over, the doctor asked to speak with my mother and me in his office privately. As if I were invisible, he told my mother that he thought I was suicidal. He based his theory on the fact that I had been crying the entire time he shined a light and stuck things in my vagina in a room full of people. My mother argued that I was a fifteen-year-old girl who just found out she was pregnant. Crying, my mother said, seemed an appropriate reaction. When the time came to find a pediatrician, she again took me to one that she knew. Dr. Gregory was the one who had finally been the one to diagnose my sister Allison with Prader-Willi Syndrome ten years earlier. My mother thought highly of him because of this and it was his office where my sisters and I had received all our childhood shots and physicals.

My mother wanted us to talk to him about the situation and set it up so that after the baby arrived it could become a patient of his. Dr. Gregory took the opportunity to explain to me what a horrible person I was to have done this to my family, how embarrassed they all were. He said every other horrible thing you could say to someone already paying a life sentence for a three-second mistake. My mother interrupted him and told him that *she* was my parent and she was not there for him to speak to me that way.

We left and never went back.

One night, not long after that, I was almost asleep when I heard the door to my room creak open and the light from the hall began to filter in. My father sat on the bed beside me and held my hand. Choking back tears, he told me he was scared that I wouldn't be able to do all of the things I was meant to do. I squeezed his hand and told him that I wouldn't let this stop me even if it slowed me down. I promised him I would be everything I ever could be and that I would never use this baby as an excuse to not be or do anything.

The few months that followed were difficult. My parents, usually very social, spent time at home on the couch in each other's arms. I tried my very best to be invisible. We fought about the things I was and was not allowed to do. Despite my condition I was still a fifteen-year-old girl. I received my learner's permit during that time and would get my driver's license just six weeks before the baby. I felt I should be given some freedom before I gave it up for the next eighteen years. My parents, on the other hand, thought I needed to be out of the public eye.

I didn't find out the sex of the baby. Not because I didn't want to know, but because during the ultrasound I was too embarrassed to ask—and they didn't ask if I wanted to know. The baby appeared to be healthy, and I was on track for my July 2 due date. Everyone predicted I would be having an Independence Day baby.

They were right. I went into labor on July 3 as fireworks went off outside my hospital window. James Tyler was born at 5 a.m. on July 4. I named him James after my dad but called him by his middle name, Tyler—a weird Southern tradition.

I started my junior year of high school that September, two months into motherhood. The walls that had never quite felt welcoming now felt even less familiar than before. The people I used to know didn't know how to talk to me or how to be my friend. They didn't know how to explain to their own parents that I had a baby at home. They cared about dating and parties and cars. I was only allowed to care about work, car seats, and diapers.

My parents were the best parents possible in that situation. They tried their best to help me without taking my responsibility away. They wanted a very clear understanding that the baby was my responsibility but they would help when I needed it. This was difficult, made no easier by the fact that I was now a sixteen-year-old who didn't know how not to take advantage of the situation. I wanted my mom to babysit Tyler and they wanted me to babysit my little sisters.

Eventually I got a sitter to keep Tyler during the day while I went to school. This significantly improved my relationship with my mom, but for the rest of our lives my son has always been stuck somewhere between being my child and my little brother. My parents were forty when I made them grandparents and they still had two small children of their own; my youngest sister just ten years old. Strangers always assumed my son was my brother. We never corrected them.

My story of being a teen mom is not a good one. I did not give birth to my best friend. I was not made better because of it, or stronger. If I could go back and talk to my younger pregnant self, I would tell her to have an abortion or give the baby up for adoption. Or better yet, to trust her instincts and stay as far away as possible from sex until she was much older and better prepared for the emotions and consequences that come with it. It would take 20 years for anyone to say to me that I had survived, and thrived, despite my situation. It took 20 years for me to say it, too. I graduated from high school on time, with my son on my hip. I was accepted to Virginia Commonwealth University and was on the waiting list for the engineering school at Virginia Tech. I had decided I wanted to be an architect or an engineer and both would require a formal degree. Ready to be the grown up I felt like I already was, I accepted my invitation to VCU and set off for a new life two hours away from my parents, baby in tow.

I failed miserably. I lived off campus with just Tyler at first. Kelly and I had long since become friends again and she ended up living with me for a short stint, too, but that did not go well. I hated school, suffered severe depression, overspent on credit cards, and failed almost all my classes. After a year, I was ready to go home. I was completely deflated. I wanted to prove to everyone that the baby hadn't ruined my life and that I was capable of taking care of myself, but I was still just a kid trying to figure out who I was and how to become the adult I was expected to be. Having a child matured me in some ways, but it did not speed up my development. A seventeen-year-old mother is still a seventeen-year-old girl.

Still, I had hope that I would be more than a teen mom. I had an unwavering belief that I was meant for something bigger. I wanted to write books and I wanted to be famous. The baby at first felt like an obstacle but later turned out to be what made me different from everyone else. It gave me a story worth telling.

Paul and I had fallen into a cyclic rhythm of breaking up and getting back together. When I returned home, tail between my legs, we reunited. After getting somewhat back on my feet and getting my own apartment he secretly moved in. We felt sort of like a real family—except he didn't work, preferring to stay up all night playing video games. He was terribly mean to me. But that Christmas, next to the tree, he proposed. I said yes. I was only eighteen, to be married at nineteen.

He was still that overprotective, jealous, depressed kid. He didn't know how to control his emotions. I was scared of him and for him. Our wedding was set for that July. Luckily my lease was up before then and I convinced him it would be best if I moved back in with my parents before the wedding to save money. I was so scared to tell my parents about how bad it was. Finally, my best friend at the time, Michelle, threatened to tell them if I didn't. I broke down and told my mom. She wasn't angry at all, even though we already had invitations, dresses, and the wedding was only 30 days away. I don't really know what she was. Perhaps a bit relieved her young daughter wasn't getting married at 19 like she had? Or disappointed since marrying my son's father would have brought a sense of right-doing in God's eyes and hers, too.

I was able to break things off for the last time with Paul over the phone. He still showed up and threatened to kill himself. He told our son he was going to heaven and to always remember it was my fault. It took a strength I didn't know I had to finally realize I couldn't fix him no matter how much I cared. You can't love someone out of depression. What followed in our relationship was court dates, child support, custody battles and hell for almost the next decade.

CHAPTER THREE

No matter how many times Paul and I tried to make it work, my heart still belonged to Justin. After everything I had been through I was still a hopeless romantic that believed my heart couldn't be wrong. But I was fighting my internal demons—and societal norms—that kept trying to convince me to be with the father of my child. Life was supposed to be better with Paul. We could be a "real" family. It felt like my sins would be forgiven if I could just dedicate the rest of my life to someone I didn't love for the sake of my child. It was what was best for my son, I was told. Mothers did what was best for their children, not themselves. And so I carried a new burden: The guilt I felt by not wanting to date or marry Paul, into my twenties.

I remember exactly where I was the day I ran into Justin for the first time after all those years. Michelle and I had taken a journey to Chick-Fil-A when I saw him getting out of his car. In just a moment my nerves returned, and I immediately sweated through my shirt. We had spoken on the phone a few times since he graduated but hadn't seen each other, though I never quit thinking about him. I had to talk to him.

My friendship with Michelle had become the most important relationship of my short life. She had seen me through everything that had happened since I was thirteen. She was unwavering in her love and support for me and, more importantly, she was honest with me. She told me when I was screwing up but didn't judge whether I took her advice or not. Our friendship felt different than all the others. I could talk to her about absolutely anything. She calmed me when I was upset, laughed with me every chance she got, and stood beside me when my life spiraled. We had bonded around the age of fourteen over many things but mostly because we felt our fathers were exactly the same. She was one of the only friends I had that never turned her back on me for a second when I was pregnant.

Michelle, my greatest confidante, was not a fan of Justin. She did not think I should talk to him.

I talked to him anyway. We approached him slowly, cautiously. It had taken so much time for me to get over our last fiasco and she did not want to see me fall into that rabbit hole again. Me, I couldn't wait. Justin and I started talking again daily and before long we had what I considered to be a relationship. He was fresh back from a few years in college and seemed so much more mature than he had been. He had a "real job" and seemed to be doing well.

When I was 20, I moved into a house with a friend of mine, Kyle. He was a great roommate and I look back on the year we lived there with incredible fondness. He tolerated me and my five-year-old. He did not, however, tolerate my "boyfriend." I use that term loosely, as Justin would not call me his girlfriend. We spoke daily, hung out most days, and were sleeping together. And yet, I guess I was still not good enough.

The duplex we were renting had one parking space in the back. If you were not in that spot you had to find parking on the street. Justin didn't like that. When he came to visit he would instead park in our front yard. Every time he did, we got in trouble with our landlady. Kyle and I asked him to stop, but his response was always: "Fuck her" (the landlady). He continued to do it. His 4Runner would leave horrible tire tracks and completely ruin the yard. Justin didn't care. He never cared about how his actions affected others.

I hated myself for letting him back into my life, over and over again. But I didn't know how to stop. Sadly, you can't change the way you feel. I was a 21-year-old girl with a five-year-old child. I carried that shame around on my back daily. I thought then that Justin was better than I deserved.

As the months passed by I thought things were getting better between us. Soon, Christmas time was upon us. Justin was working for a company his aunt owned in the IT department. I was going to the local community college and working at a bank. We had fallen into a pretty normal routine. We had a small group of friends that hung out regularly. We did the same thing all the time. Same bars, same clubs, every weekend.

A couple of days before Christmas Eve he wasn't answering his phone. He ended up calling later in the night from a bathroom at a club that we sometimes went to and told me he was out with some friends from work. This had never happened before. I got a sharp pain in my gut and I just knew he was with another woman. I asked him questions and he avoided answering them. He called me later that night—very late—saying he had given someone from work a ride home and was on his way back and just wanted to check in. I knew.

I did not want to know.

On Christmas Eve he called to tell me that he had met a girl from work. She was 18 and they had been seeing each other for several weeks. Her name was Sherry. I was devastated. Ever the gentleman, Justin continued to call me each night after he dropped her off. He would pretend like he was coming home from somewhere else and try to talk to me all the way home. I continued to hang up on him and tell him to leave me alone. At the time, Sherry seemed like a child. Justin was twenty-four. It seemed almost gross that he would be dating an eighteen-year-old.

That was one horrible, horrible Christmas. I remember going to my aunt's house and sitting silently beside one of my cousins and trying desperately to not cry. What kind of person breaks up with his girlfriend on Christmas Eve? The kind of person that I was still involved with after almost 10 years. The kind of man I couldn't walk away from. As was customary, I was very mad. I stopped talking to him. I never wanted to see him again. The problem was we shared friends. I knew I needed to get away from Justin but I didn't know how. I considered moving in with my grandparents in another state. I considered moving home. Michelle was living in an apartment with her boyfriend in the same city about fifteen minutes away. She offered to let my son and me come stay with them while I figured out what I was doing. So I did. I lived with her and her boyfriend in their one-bedroom apartment for a short time until they upgraded to a two-bedroom. Then the apartment adjacent to theirs became available and I moved in.

Living next door to my best friend was a dream come true. With Michelle's help I was able to attend IT classes and get Microsoft certified which led me to my first well-paying job. I was working 10-hour shifts four days a week, and Michelle and her boyfriend helped me with Tyler whenever they could. We sat outside together while Tyler played, chatted over breakfast, and got to spend so much time together. It was as close as I ever got to dorm life.

That's where I was living when Justin decided that Sherry wasn't for him and he wanted me back. He made me a mixtape which, up to that point, was the only nice thing that he'd ever done for me. I'll never forget that he had heard Dido and decided I would like her. He brought me her CD, too. Slowly we started to become friends again. My argument with him was that I was tired of playing games. I already had one child and if I was going to start a family, I wanted to get married and do it before my son got too old. I wanted my kids to be close together. Tyler was already six.

At a barbecue our friends had thrown, Justin asked if he could talk to me. We went into a room alone and he presented me with a diamond ring. It was not an engagement ring, but it certainly could have been. He gave it to me and promised that it meant that he was done with the bullshit, and he was all in. But the diamond ring did it. I was an unwed mother. I wanted to get married to make my sin less obvious, less heavy. If I was married, nobody would know my son didn't belong to my husband. I saw getting married as a way to atone for my sins, a get-out-of-jail-free card. I believed wholeheartedly that in order to give me that ring he had to be ready to really be with me and that he had realized I was the "one". We were back together.

While living in the apartment next to Michelle, I had taken classes through Microsoft, received my certifications, and had been hired at a new job in a call center helping people set up or fix their high speed internet connections. I was making real money for the first time in my life. I decided that it was time for me to start looking into buying a house. After much thought I decided to move back to the town where I had grown up as it seemed the best place to raise children. I was beyond ready to settle down and not feel the sting of single motherhood.

Justin proposed to me on a cold day in January. We went to the beach. It was freezing.

I remember everything about the room at the motel where we stayed. We walked outside into the cool air on the balcony and as I looked out at the ocean, he came up behind me and wrapped his arms around me to keep me warm. Then, he told me to put my hand in his coat pocket. When I did, I found a ring box. I remember the cold wind whipping me in the face.

He did not go down on one knee. He celebrated our new engagement by getting completely wasted, just the two of us in a motel room. I remember calling my parents to tell them. The moment after becoming engaged I looked at the calendar and realized my parent's anniversary was on a Saturday. I decided instantly that I wanted to get married on their anniversary, March 31. I had twelve weeks to plan a wedding. Luckily, this was not my first attempt.

Planning the wedding was a reality check. I was amazed beyond measure that my parents were still willing to pay for it after all I had put them through. Justin wanted to make every single decision. I wanted to get married on the beach. Justin, who was not religious, wanted to get married in a church. Even then it felt wrong to get married in a church to someone who did not go to church. I had always dreamt about getting married outside, it was not to be. My mother smirked at Justin's insistence that he be the one to choose the flowers.

My mom and I went to buy my dress. To prove how nonchalant I was about the entire thing, I picked out a $99 dress off the rack. I didn't care. While trying the dress on I realized how cute it was with my white platform tennis shoes. The dress looked like something Cinderella would wear. The bodice was fitted and the skirt looked like a huge bell. You could not see my shoes. I decided I wanted to wear my tennis shoes at the wedding. I thought it was so me. When I told Justin, he was furious. He thought it was trashy, awful, and not how people got married. But nothing about me had been traditional, and I didn't think our wedding was a good time to start. But here we were, planning out our traditional wedding in a church, with my traditional wedding gown, and the flowers he picked out. It started to feel as though this was not our wedding, it was his.

What I remember most about my wedding day is the feeling I had after he and I said our vows and walked to the back of the church alone. I turned and looked at him and he looked at me, and neither of us had anything to say. We did not smile, we did not laugh, and we did not embrace. I realized right then that much of our relationship was either bad, or it was us hanging out with our friends and having fun. It hit me then that the two of us together might not be that great. I turned twenty-three six weeks later.

I had always wanted my kids to be close in age. We decided to start trying for a child right away. My mother and I fought about this. She didn't understand why I wouldn't wait a while and enjoy my marriage. To me, the only reason we got married was because we wanted to have kids. I didn't see the point in waiting. It took nine months to get pregnant. I found out in January, almost exactly a year after we got engaged.

Red flags continued to pop up in my marriage to Justin. He expected me to do all the laundry, iron his clothes, do the grocery shopping and be the sole caretaker for our children. Even though I, too, was working full time, he wanted the traditional marriage our parents had experienced. I was expected to be the perfect stay-at-home mom while working full time (and making more money than he did). We moved into our first home the same month we married and at the age of 22, I became a homeowner and wife—and I was already a mother.

It was nothing for Justin to stay up until four or five o'clock in the morning on weekends. He loved Jim Beam, and I couldn't believe how late he could stay up drinking it. He liked to stay up late during the weeknights too, so I went to bed alone. Finding out that I was pregnant with his baby changed absolutely nothing. I woke up one day at 5 a.m. and discovered that Justin was nowhere to be found. My cousin lived down the street and I figured his house was the only place he could be. I walked there. When I arrived, I found him passed out on the couch. I kicked him, I hit him, I took his keys to the house. I was really over it. I was also pregnant.

I had hoped the birth of our child would change my husband's behavior. I was, of course, very, very wrong.

Justin wanted to name our son after his dying grandfather, whose name was James. Justin wanted to name our new baby James Earl Gray.

For starters, I said, Earl Grey is a kind of tea. Second of all, James Earl Ray—just one letter from our son's name—assassinated Martin Luther King, Jr. And third, and I would argue, most importantly, I already had a child named James. We fought until after my son was born. Justin refused to compromise. "*I* don't have a kid named James," he said.

My son was named James Hatteras Earl Gray. And I now had two kids with the same first name. We called our son Hatteras, the name I loved, But I would never forgive Justin for making me name him James.

Having Hatteras at home was one of the most joyous times of my life. I couldn't get enough of him. He was the most beautiful child I'd ever seen. I can honestly say I was happier then than I had ever been before. He was a dream come true for me. I wanted four more exactly like him.

I had now been through two pregnancies and two births and they could not have been more different. The first pregnancy I spent crying and trying to hide my baby bump. I didn't know the sex and I got to pick the name all by myself. The second pregnancy I spent crying tears of joy, wearing maternity clothes, and fighting over the name. Everyone was excited for my second child and we celebrated pregnancy milestones and had happy baby showers and decorated a nursery. The second time I was married and doing it "right." I was married to the person who I lost my virginity to, which somehow appeased God in my mind. I was finally living my life the way I was "supposed to." I still had two children with two different fathers and I was still young by today's standards, but I was following the rules. People were proud of me and loved to tell me so. I did it!

After Hatteras was born, Justin and I started looking for a bigger house. We found our dream home and bought it for a deal. The owner had been renting it and the renters trashed it. We cleaned it up. We moved from a 1,400 square-foot house to a 2,400 square-foot house with a pool. For a while things were great. I was over the moon in love with my son. Our new house was beautiful. But one thought stopped me in my tracks: I was 25 years old and I already had everything I was supposed to want.

I was living someone else's dream.

And sure, I did have some of the things that I had wanted my whole life. I had a husband. I had my two kids. I had my beautiful house with a pool and a white picket fence. I had a great job. I was working towards a degree. I should have been ecstatic.

And yet, I was living in hell.

Justin did not help with the baby. Justin did not help with anything. The baby didn't sleep through the night until he was nine months old. I was so tired. I would beg Justin to get up with him just one day, so I could get some sleep. He absolutely refused. He also rarely changed diapers. He would casually take naps on the couch while I ran around with two kids. He didn't give them baths. And he certainly didn't make meals. I'd started to really resent him.

And then things got worse. Family pictures were a must for happy families and I had dreamt about my own. I was excited to schedule family pictures of my own family, I wanted to see my family depicted the way I felt we were. But Justin decided he would rather go fishing with his friends than take photos with his family. So I took the pictures alone with my kids. It was a sad foreshadowing of my future.

A few months later, I fell violently ill. I was vomiting every half hour for seven hours. This was rare for me—I almost never got sick enough to throw up. Justin had a friend in town and needed to give him a ride home, about an hour away. He said he was going to give him a ride and come right back. I explained that I was in no shape to take care of a baby and pleaded for his help. He was infuriated that he would have to take Hatteras, but he did.

Imagine my surprise when he returned, eight hours later, friend still in tow. After a day of drinking with my son, they decided they had been out long enough that they could bring him home, drop him off, and head back out. I was still retching. In front of his friends I told him he could not leave me alone with a baby while I was this sick. I could barely get up. He cussed and yelled until his friend Brad agreed to take the out-of-town friend home. Then, Justin sat on the other sofa and told me, without an ounce of sarcasm, to make him a sandwich. Right then, in that one sentence I saw what my future would look like if I stayed. I saw that this was truly who he was—selfishness was so woven into the fabric of his character, that it was *him*. I remembered sitting on his bed as a teenager, watching him tell his mother to get the fuck out of his room and make him a sandwich. *If I stayed, I would become her. I feared my sons would repeat the cycle that Justin and his brothers had created. I knew that I needed to start formulating a plan to get out.*

I knew I had to leave Justin once and for all after a trip he took to Myrtle Beach, South Carolina, for a friend's bachelor party. He left on Thursday and planned to come back on Sunday. At midnight that Thursday, his paycheck hit our bank account. It was earmarked for our mortgage. By the time I awoke on Friday, Justin's entire paycheck had been spent at a strip club.

Panicked, I called him over and over. Surely his card had to have been stolen. Surely the strip club had overcharged him. Something had to be very wrong. I was briefly concerned that he was dead. When I finally got him on the phone, Justin said, "How was I supposed to pay for it?"

He did not apologize. He was not even concerned about finding the money to pay the mortgage for the house where his wife and family lived. I was already fantasizing about leaving, but once this happened I realized that I needed to take those thoughts more seriously.

I was so tired. Tired of not sleeping. Tired of being the only person in the house who ever handled anything. Tired of being the person who had to go to bed early and had to get up early to take care of the kids. Tired of being the only one in the house to have any responsibility. Tired of going to bed alone, tired of spending my mornings alone with the kids, and sick and tired of the lies and deceit. It dawned on me that my two boys would have this man as their role model. It was important to me that they learn to take responsibility for their actions, to hold their family in high regard, and to work together in relationships as a team. All things they were not witnessing in our home.

I tried so hard to leave. I went and stayed with my parents for a few days. I tried to tell them how unhappy I was, but I was too scared to tell them about all the other things. I'm sure that they knew there was more to the story but I couldn't tell them the truth. I couldn't tell them that I hated him and he repulsed me. I had no respect for him as a person. I was embarrassed and ashamed, again. They told me that marriage was hard. That I had made my bed and I needed to sleep in it. They told me, "You don't leave your husband. You don't get divorced." Living up to what society expected of me was killing me, again.

How could I promise to spend the rest of my life with someone I didn't love or respect? How could living in this hell make me a "good" mother and show I had a "successful" marriage? How could I promise a lifetime of having sex with someone that made me feel degraded, easily replaceable, and disgusting? I returned home to try again. It was one of the biggest mistakes of my life. I wish by then I had learned to trust myself and my instincts.

I knew without a doubt that I was done for the rest of my life with Justin. I did not love him. I despised him. I hated it every time my phone rang and I saw that it was him. Sure, he had done some awful things, but I hated him the most for turning me into someone I no longer recognized. I could not let my boys grow up with this man as a role model or with me as the person Justin had turned me into. I was awful. I yelled, I screamed, I cried. I threw things, I hit him. Anger was becoming a part of me; more than just a fleeting feeling and more like a constant companion.

I wish I had stayed gone the first time because when I came back, I slowly began falling in love with our friend Brad. Brad was at our house a lot, almost always on our couch. Brad would get up in the morning and help me with the kids. He would do everything around the house that seemed to keep piling up. He fixed the broken drawer Justin had been ignoring. When I became frustrated he would take the kids outside to play. All the while my husband would sleep until three o'clock in the afternoon. Brad and I became close friends. He would talk to me about the girls he was dating. Sometimes he would ask for advice. He saw where Justin was lacking, and he tried to help. Then, Justin quit his job. For six months he did not apply for a single job and spent every day "working on his resume." Every day I got up and took our son to daycare, went to work, then picked him up and came home. It never occurred to Justin that perhaps he should take care of his son during the day so we could save money on daycare. I lost all respect for him. Physically, he repulsed me. On Valentine's Day I told Justin for at least the third time that I did not want to be married anymore. We had had that awful conversation several times before, and he just thought if he helped with the laundry or changed a diaper or two I would get over it. I didn't. I told him that I did not want to do anything for the upcoming Valentine's Day because we were not together anymore. I had already started looking for a new place to live and had found one. I had a house that I was going to rent beginning March 1. For Valentine's Day he bought me a gift and covered our bed in roses. He was still not listening. I couldn't keep having the same conversation over and over again. I told him that until I moved out we should take turns spending the weekend with the kids so one of us could go do something else and give one another space. On one particular weekend he was supposed to be gone Friday night and back on Saturday night. He was supposed to relieve the babysitter that I had. It was Michelle's birthday, and Erin and I went out to meet her to celebrate.

I left the bar that night with Brad. I did not go home until the next morning. Shock waves went through the bar, through our friends, and through my husband when he heard. I did not care. I did not sleep a wink that night, but I also did not sleep with Brad. I had emotional feelings for him, which I did not know how to change, but our relationship was not sexual.

Erin went to the house the following morning and picked up Tyler. She walked the Justin minefield and made sure that Tyler was safe and tried to establish some peace. When I came home to face Justin later that day, I told him the truth. I told him that I was not coming home. He asked me if I loved Brad and I said yes. I told him that I had had feelings for him for a long time. I also told him that we both knew this marriage was not working. It should have been no surprise that Justin took absolutely no responsibility for the state of our marriage. It was easier to blame it all on Brad even though we were in a terrible place long before things changed between Brad and me. I was faced once again with a moral dilemma. I didn't want to feel this way about Brad, but I did. In the end I chose to tell my husband the truth and leave before things escalated. It was of no consequence.

Justin broke every glass in the house. Champagne glasses, wine glasses, coffee cups; gone. Whenever our phone rang he answered it and told the person on the other line that I was a whore. He told this to my uncle, my cousin, and several friends. Thankfully, our son was staying with Justin's parents for the time being. I knew this, but he did not know I knew this, so he continued to tell me that he had our son and that I didn't need to know where he was or worry about him anymore. I remained calm. I knew my son was in good hands with his grandparents, so I didn't fight him on it. I refused to let Justin use our son as a pawn. He did everything he could to try and hurt me. I was grateful Tyler was safe with his grandmother for all of this.

Looking back, it was naïve to think our relationship was starting from scratch when we got married. All of that baggage, thirteen years of hurt and heartbreak, followed its way into our home. Justin, in his defense, had been the same person all along. Why wouldn't he be? I felt I should have known what I was walking into—and I must have, on some level, but I ignored it, pushed it down, and just kept walking into the lion's den.

I've never once cried about my marriage since I left. Nor do I really feel like I did something wrong, though I know that's not the way I am "supposed" to feel. Growing up, I hadn't understood that married women could have feelings for people who aren't their husbands. I was taught that when you get married you only have feelings for your husband for the rest of your life. So, when I found myself having feelings for someone who wasn't Justin, I took it to mean I wasn't like everyone else. It was yet another thing separating me from everyone I knew. Finally, after thirteen years, I put myself unapologetically first, an act which went against my entire upbringing. Nevertheless, I did not feel bad at all. I felt Justin had lied to me, snuck around behind my back, and treated me like garbage for way too long. He deserved worse.

My freedom came at a high price. But then I began to really sleep. I began to wake up with a smile on my face, happy to be alive. I began to enjoy my children more because I wasn't simultaneously infuriated with Justin being asleep or not helping. I was no longer sleeping in a bed trying desperately not to be touched. I felt safe in my environment. Inside my home everything was perfect, but outside those walls it was still chaos.

I lost almost all of my friends and much of my family. Getting divorced was bad enough, but everyone believing that I had an affair made things worse. My parents were sad, angry, and embarrassed (again). The rumors flying around were plentiful. Some said that I had been cheating for years and Hatteras was Brad's son. All of them assumed Brad and I had slept together, which we had not. Desperate for an explanation, my circle of loved ones thought I must be on drugs. Everyone thought I had lost my mind.

My phone went silent. No one called to check on me. Of my 25 first cousins, only one reached out to see if I was okay. The two that I hung out with almost every week chose Justin. They told me they completely understood me divorcing Justin, but they had a problem with me dating Brad. Nonetheless I felt like I didn't need anyone else—I had Brad. Brad told me I was beautiful, all the time. When he messed up, which he did often, he owned up to it and was full of apologies and flowers. He took responsibility for his actions, which I found refreshing. He helped me put together beds in my new place. He would bring over dinner and help me cook. In short, he went out of his way to help me, to do nice things for me, and he made me very happy. Never before had someone treated me like they were lucky to know me. The kids still only knew Brad as a friend, of course. He had always been around before, so it was not weird for him to be around now. He didn't spend the night (though he did leave very late, often) and we didn't express our feelings in front of the kids until much later.

Justin and I sold our house in one day. We made a great deal of money, which we split. I bought my own house. I also bought a boat. I got my surname back. Life felt like it was finally falling into place for me. When I wasn't dealing with the repercussions of the divorce, I was happy.

We split all of our assets in half, we each kept our cars, and we decided on 50/50 custody. There was no child support or alimony. He got to keep most of what was in the house, furniture wise, and he sold the few things I did want. If I said I wanted something, Justin made sure I wouldn't get it. He took both computers and all the pictures contained on the hard drives. He took our china, our wedding albums, and after much arguing, he took back my wedding ring. It took years for me to get back the videos my parents had made of my sisters and me when we were kids. He kept Hatteras' birth certificate and social security card. I didn't even mention it, I just got copies.

Living up to the expectations I thought had been set for me early in life was slowly destroying me. As I approached 26, a single mom of two boys with two different fathers, I really had to look inside and decide what expectations I was going to set for myself. I started a new list of my own. The most important things on it were my kids and me. Time after time I faced challenges that forced me to question my true self, my beliefs, and how far I was willing to go to make everyone else happy. It was strange to think that while no one knew what was really going on in my life, they judged me for whatever they believed no matter how hard I tried to live up to their expectations. It made no sense. The only standards I could possibly live up to were my own. If I wanted to be proud of who I was, I had to make decisions I could be proud of. I needed to own my life and all of the twists and turns thus far.

CHAPTER FOUR

The rules of parenting completely changed after my divorce. Once I finally settled into sharing my sons 50/50 with both of their fathers, what followed were the best parenting years I ever had. I loved my weeks with the kids and I loved my weeks without them. Having been a mom since I was 16, I found that the week without kids gave me my first taste of adulthood and freedom. I was able to pretend I was young and carefree, albeit for a limited time. The week I had my kids I was much more able to enjoy parenting. Cooking dinner every night wasn't so daunting one week at a time.

I learned to co-parent, making a conscious effort to raise my children with my norms and values while also respecting the norms and values their fathers brought. First, I learned how to co-parent Tyler with Paul's mother, then with Paul, and then with Paul and his new wife. Then, when Justin and I divorced, I co-parented with him and then later his new wife. Everything I planned that involved my kids involved coordinating with both of their dads. That part was not easy.

Over the years, I have fought about nearly every issue under the sun with my co-parenting partners. I fought to keep my eight-year-old from being able to play mature video games. I fought over meeting spots, laundry, school systems, bed times, wake up times, being home alone, vacations, birthdays, holidays and even food. I was once accused of not feeding my son because he was small (it took an endocrinologist's opinion to prove that he was just small, not malnourished). It sometimes felt like the fights would never stop.

After the divorce Justin was forced to take some responsibility for Hatteras and thankfully he stepped up to the plate. He was motivated by his desire to appear as the "good" parent and make me look awful. He had already convinced everyone that he was the victim of an affair, so it seemed fitting that I would also be an absent mom. He made people pity him and if I am being honest, I pitied him, too.

But regardless of his motives, Justin signed up to be the soccer coach for several years. He was insistent on being at every teacher conference and doctor's appointment. I am not sure if he turned into a good dad to spite me or if he had it in him all along, but in the end Hatteras had a present and involved dad and I couldn't have been happier. As a single dad, Justin impressed me. As a co-parent he disappointed me, despite me thinking it was impossible for him to disappoint me more than he already had. For a while I was embarrassed at his insistence on being around. Neither he nor I was brought up with a father who was very present. I thought two parents were definitely not needed for childhood checkups or most teacher meetings, but it didn't hurt. Our week on, week off schedule often landed with the first day of school at Justin's. At first, I was sad not to be a part of it—but then I realized how hectic and crazy that first week could be, how much paperwork had to be filled out, signed and returned, and I learned to embrace the second week. There was one year, however, when I reached out to a teacher when Hatteras was having so much trouble, only to find out that she didn't know I existed. Justin had left all of my information and contact info off the forms at the beginning of the year. This way, he could make sure he had the power to decide which parts I should be a part of, and which I should not. I could have confronted him about this, but instead I started sending in a note on that second week explaining our shared custody and including my email and phone number. The teachers never had any issue with adding both of our emails to any correspondence.

I ordered copies of Hatteras' social security card and birth certificate, since Justin had taken our originals. He was surprised when I said I could sign our son up for soccer without a problem. "They need his birth certificate," he said.

"I know. I've got it," I replied.

I had just avoided a fight.

When Justin and I first separated we tried several versions of shared custody but ultimately landed on week on/week off switching to Mondays. We tried switching on Sundays for a long time, too, but I realized I woke up every Sunday filled with anxiety because I had to see my ex-husband who still tried to make me miserable. He would always show up late if at all. Once Hatteras started preschool we moved to Mondays and our lives improved dramatically. One Monday I would put him on the bus or drop him off at school and Justin would get him that afternoon. Then we would switch. It eliminated tons of arguing.

We legally filed for joint shared custody and agreed to split medical and educational expenses. Neither of us went after any form of child support. When we separated Justin had been out of work for six months. He spent the next six months living with his parents and looking for a job. Not only was child support something he couldn't afford, it was something I wasn't interested in regardless.

It had been different with Paul—I fought with him for child support for years. I hated that I had to work and raise Tyler while Paul got to do whatever he wanted. He got new cars, went unemployed for long periods of time, and always seemed to have excuses for missing court dates or being there when I needed him. I saw what it did to our relationship and to Tyler, and I didn't want that for Hatteras or for me. I found it difficult, if not impossible, to separate the child support due and the time he got to spend with his child—even though I believed it was wrong to keep a child from one of its parents over money. I understood that a child should see his father no matter what but I struggled to separate that from the feeling that he needed to earn his right to be with his son.

So much of parenting for me had been fighting with Paul. It was the default that Tyler was with me—we had to schedule time for him to be with Paul. This meant that for me, life revolved around being a parent, but for Paul, parenting revolved around life. He could plan to pick up Tyler around his work schedule, social life, grocery store runs, or errands. To me those things all had to happen *with* a child. It seemed so incredibly unfair. His parenting responsibility ended with the $300 a month he was supposed to provide, and he couldn't even do that most of the time. Add to it that I did not want to be a parent, did not want to be working, paying babysitters, or going to school. If it had been acceptable in society and our roles were reversed, I would probably have done exactly what he did. He got to cling to some parts of his youth and embrace parenthood when he was ready. I did not.

I was glad Justin wanted to be a more present father than Paul—but sometimes he was too present. He wanted to call and talk to Hatteras every night. He would call at random times, never knowing if we were in the middle of dinner or a movie. I would hate it when Justin started calling while I was trying to get dinner on the table and the kids were finishing their homework. When Hatteras got a bad grade, it was magnified—I would reprimand him, and then Justin would reprimand him twice. After a while, I told him that he needed to stop calling. Hatteras was with me and he was fine. He didn't need two parents every night to ask how his day was, two parents to yell at him to do his homework.

I did my best not to bother Hatteras when he was at his dad's house. That was a tough adjustment but was something that I got used to. I knew that I had to trust Justin to do the bare-minimum of co-parenting and accept that it was okay if Hatteras' routine there wasn't identical to the one at my house. So long as he was being fed, bathed, and getting his homework done it was all going to be fine.

Just like all boys, mine managed to destroy their clothes and shoes at a rate I could barely comprehend. Their rooms were always messy, food only *sometimes* made it all the way into their mouths, and if it wasn't dirty, it was probably lost. I had heated conversations with their fathers about who bought what, whose house it got to go to, and who replaced things. According to Paul, he and his wife would buy Tyler very nice new clothes which would then disappear and be replaced with the "crap" I bought him. I wouldn't have any idea how this was happening. Once, Tyler's step-mom and his dad showed up to go through all of Tyler's clothes and "take back" what was "theirs." We were at my parents' house and the kids were playing in the pool when Paul and his wife insisted on coming over right then. It put Tyler—and my parents—in a very uncomfortable position. To avoid further conflict, we allowed them to go through Tyler's chest of drawers and take what they thought was theirs. I imagine in that moment Tyler must have felt that nothing was truly his.

I found it incredibly frustrating that my children were learning that gifts came with rules and restrictions. They were just starting to become individuals who wanted certain shoes or certain brands and to develop their own styles. They would be so excited to receive the new shoes they wanted on Sunday only to be told they couldn't wear them for a week until they returned the following Monday. I hated it for them. I knew it was hard on them but there was nothing I could do to make their fathers see what they were doing so I had to do the best I could and just not restrict the things I bought them.

I still don't understand how this happened. My son would leave in one outfit and return in another. How in the world would all of his underwear end up at one house? How did he run out of pants? From time to time he would have a favorite hoodie or pair of shoes that we realized he was taking back and forth in his backpack but I could not ever explain the frequency in which the clothes got misplaced.

It wasn't just clothes. We fought about gaming systems, laptops, games, and seasons passes. One thing we fought about was seasons passes to an amusement park. The pass was bought for my son but if I wanted to take him I wasn't "allowed" to use it. How awful that my son was put in a situation where he had to see such pettiness. It would have cost nothing for Hatteras to use it, and he would have gotten to use his gift more. I couldn't see how that was not a win-win.

While the arguments I had with my sons' fathers were numerous, without a doubt my largest co-parenting challenges came from their new wives, mostly Paul's.

Those women were fierce. I never got to the co-parenting dream land where I was friends with either of them. I failed miserably at ever trying to connect with them and get to a place where we could talk openly about my children. I first met Paul's new wife at a hearing on child support—a situation which doesn't lend itself to friendly encounters. We were all taken into a small room to turn over our W-2's so the court could determine the amount each of us should pay. Seething, Ann turned to me and said, "I am the breadwinner in this family." I kept my silence, not sure how to respond.

To this day I am not sure how she thought it would affect me or what that had to do with child support, but it was just a glimpse of the rest of our relationship.

I made it through 50/50 parenting of both of my children, watching them both graduate from high school as well as turn eighteen and start their adult lives. I'd like to think that I got better at it as time progressed. Along the way I established some go-to questions that I used to help guide me when things got tough and I needed to respond to something:

How will this text/email/call benefit my son?

Would I be proud of this response if I knew my child would get to read it?

Am I fighting for their lives to be better or am I increasing bitterness?

Am I killing them with kindness or pettiness?

How can I respond in a way that will make me proud and not revengeful?

Am I responding to the actual topic or to my feelings of hurt and anger?

One thing that helped me when I knew I wanted to say a lot of things I shouldn't was to write an email of exactly how I felt and NOT send it. I would write it, give myself some time, then after I got it out I found it easier to go back and respond more maturely and respectfully. This was especially helpful when Ann and I were at each other's throats about something with Tyler. Once, she made a spreadsheet that counted hours and showed percentages of time spent at each home. Now, I can see the functionality in this but then all I saw was that she had reduced my child's life to numbers on a spreadsheet. I felt it showed how emotionally disconnected she was from the whole situation. But I would have felt that way no matter what she said or did. I had so much anger at Paul and she was just an extension of that.

CHAPTER FIVE

After my divorce, I became obsessed with change. New clothes, new hair, new everything. I didn't want any part of the life I had known. To some degree I had accomplished and acquired everything I had dreamed of when I was that scared 15-year-old girl. But on the other hand, I was 26 and I had everything I had ever dreamed of—and I no longer wanted it. It wasn't enough. It wasn't the right guy. It wasn't the right home, and most importantly, it wasn't me.

I had gotten so caught up in what I felt like I was supposed to want that I lost that little girl inside of me that dreamed of big cities, writing a book, and building a life that excited and fulfilled me. I still felt like that lost and misunderstood pregnant teenager, but I had created a life that almost camouflaged my past, my sins. Even though to others I had seemingly begun to pull off a "normal" life, I still saw the real me every time I looked in the mirror. The real me was withering right in front of my face. I felt like I was harboring a fugitive. Six months after my divorce I purchased an amazing home located in a great residential neighborhood on the corner of two quiet streets. As soon as I saw the weeping willow tree in the front yard, I knew this was the place for me and my boys. I pictured them playing ball in the side yard with the other neighborhood kids and it did not disappoint. That home brought a normalcy that I hadn't realized I could provide for myself. I met the neighbors and made new friends, none of whom cared about who I had been before I moved in. It felt like a miracle to find people who accepted me right when I needed it most. I bought a boat. Brad was often an amazing partner. He loved cooking dinner, helping with the yard, and doing things with me and the kids. But he and I were not meant for the long term.

I credit Brad with saving my life and helping me rebuild the *me* that I had lost, but our relationship was still complicated. For one, the whole world was against us. The rumors had really hurt us—of course there were the ones about our alleged sordid affair, but that wasn't the end of it. Some of our friends whispered that I had been on drugs, others said that Brad was the real father of my son, not Justin. Justin himself fueled the rumors—he loved the attention he received by playing the victim. None of these were true. I felt like I was walking around our small town with a scarlet A on my chest.

Rumors aside, I was older with two kids and Brad was just barely getting into adulthood. I was 26 and he was 23 but we were worlds apart. He was still partying every chance he got and I had a family and a mortgage to worry about. It took us two years to end it for good.

The best thing that came out of our relationship was my realization that I kept dating people that needed considerable help. They needed mental and emotional help that I just couldn't provide. I realized that I needed a career that would satisfy my need to help so I could focus on finding a partner—someone who felt like an equal—to share my life with. I was tired of dating people that needed me to tell them *not* to do things and what they were "allowed" to do. I was not interested in any role that resembled being a mother to them.

I still had not graduated from college. Up until that point I had dabbled in college. My single year at Virginia Commonwealth University straight out of high school had ended in disaster. Living off campus with a two-year-old was incredibly lonely and I struggled hard with depression. When I dropped out, I had only a few transferable credits. After that I tried taking some classes at the local community college but my heart wasn't in it. I still had no idea what I wanted to accomplish with my degree, so it had felt pointless until now.

I decided to major in Psychology. Now, with a real goal—and dream—in hand, I buckled down and went for that degree. I finished my associate degree through the Virginia Community College System and was accepted into Old Dominion University. When I found out I got in, I wept with joy. It felt like I had been accepted into a private society. For the first time in my life I felt validated, "good enough". I was obsessed with psychology and so it came naturally to me. I loved reading and writing about it and truly believed I had found something I could actually create my life around. I was working full time still but taking classes online and in person gave me a lot of flexibility. My mental state was much better than it had been when I was eighteen and I was determined to get my Bachelor's degree. I *had* to. I had to prove to everyone I could, including myself.

I had always held a very firm belief about abortion, that it was wrong with no exceptions, that was strong enough to make me ignore anything else political. Combine that with my Republican upbringing and I felt confident in my knowledge of right and wrong. But I was trying to become bigger than I was. I wanted to grow. To some degree I think I sought to find out why the life I had found myself in was so sinful and seemed to make so many other people uncomfortable and full of judgment. I wanted to know *more.* I wanted to know *why.* So, I began reading books that opposed my views in order to better understand the other side and, I hoped, become that much better at defending and supporting my beliefs. What I discovered shocked me.

One of the first books I read talked about the lengths that had been gone to in an effort to suppress evolution and only teach a Christian version of life. It focused mostly on George W. Bush and the decades leading up to his presidency. Even though I was a Christian, I had always thought forcing religion on others was wrong. It didn't sit right with me that significantly older white men made decisions to refute science and push their agenda. I learned more and more about abortion and the women who had died getting them unsafely—and also that women who died because they couldn't get an abortion to save their own lives. That's when I began to realize that forcing a fifteen-year-old girl to have a baby she didn't want might not be what God wanted after all. I understood why those women had risked their lives to avoid having a baby, how awful it was to have a secret that everyone would find out about. A secret you would do *anything* to hide. How had we gotten here?

Then I started researching politicians and I realized they did not practice what they preached. So many men, it seemed, were caught cheating on their wives regularly and when they begged for forgiveness, they often got it. Women were treated like second-rate citizens and called whores if they cheated or even so much as had feelings for someone else. This, too, I had learned the hard way. I finally put it together that men, who do not suffer the same in pregnancy, who can deny their paternity, skip out on financial obligations, and tell whatever lie they like, are the ones telling women they have to have the babies they don't want. And the real kicker, for me, was realizing that once a woman birthed that child she would be offered only one kind of support— welfare—and she would be crucified for using that, too! She would be judged, looked down upon, and her entire self-worth would be questioned, as if the shame of pregnancy had completely manifested itself into a new shame. This one, this new shame, crawled from the sewers when she waited in line for food stamps or paid for her food that way in the grocery stores. The injustice of it all was more than I could have ever imagined. I felt as if I was truly seeing the world for the first time. It was terrifying.

By attempting to solidify my beliefs I ended up rebuilding them all. I changed from pro-life to pro-choice. I turned into a staunch Democrat. I began to understand the benefit of a welfare system instead of assuming people were lazy or living off the government by choice. I realized that overall most people are good and are just doing the best they can. I had a new love for humanity, a new respect for individuality, and a newfound appreciation for all the people I had been taught were so different from me but were just like me in so many ways.

I was now one of the single moms I had once viewed as a different species. I was now reliant on others the way I had been taught was lazy and unacceptable. It was as if loving me *after* (after the divorce, after the "affair") was something people had to *decide* to do, and when they did stick by me, they felt as if they deserved a badge of honor for still loving someone as worthless as me. It seemed like everyone had to pick a team—they were either for me or against me. And if they chose to be on my team, they wanted accolades for sticking by me. Parents forbade their kids to talk to me. Even my younger sisters were sometimes shunned because of me. The few that publicly supported me, embraced me, and welcomed me exactly as I was, were the ones who had their own trauma, their own heartbreak, and saw through the bullshit. They had made mistakes and knew that mistakes weren't the result of a bad character or a bad life. They kept their empathy on their sleeves, not hidden away in their closets. It made me realize that all the hate in the world could be summed up with one word: unfamiliar. Once a person knew and loved someone different from themselves—a Black person, a white person, a single mom, someone struggling on welfare, someone unemployed, someone uneducated, disabled, gay, addicted to drugs—everything changed. You *got* it. Hate is just a shortened version of "I don't know anyone like that".

None of my new revelations helped me fit in again with my family, but they did something better: They made me feel whole and good and human. I felt more confident than ever to own who I was and to believe that I could be whoever I wanted to be, in spite of who I had been. I became *me*. It was glorious.

At the same time, I went completely broke. In my effort to change, I had quit my steady corporate job for a commission-only sales job that I did not succeed at. Before long, about two years after moving into my new house, my debt was overwhelming. For all the positive life changes I had undergone, this was one that I did not want. It was fortunate when a close friend of mine who had recently separated from her husband approached me with an offer I couldn't refuse. I decided to rent my house and Elly and I—and our four boys—moved in together.

We merged our lives into an old brick colonial in a new city close to Old Dominion University. Our boys shared rooms, she got the master, and I got a mother-in-law suite over the playroom. That first night, after we moved in and were sitting on the back porch with a glass of wine, it felt so right. It was so nice to have an adult to download the day with and just relax. We toasted our future, our freedom, and our new lives that seemed so brilliant and wide open. We felt like we had figured out some secret that the rest of the world wasn't privy to. We shared household responsibilities, made decisions together, sought advice and help from each other with the kids, and found the time we got just the two of us full of deep conversation and laughter. I had never had these things before.

Our weekly schedules with the boys resulted in us only having all of them twice a week. This gave us nights where it felt like our family had space, nights together that had a fun feel, and occasionally she and I had nights on our own. We met new people, found new places, and supported each other in a way I hadn't known in ages. We became L1 (her) and L2 (me). We pushed each other to get through the tough times and flourish in the good.

Things went on that way for two years. The first year was one I look back on with incredible fondness. Year two, however, was a rough one. I overstayed my welcome but had nowhere to go. Elly eventually felt like I was taking advantage of her financially. She had agreed at the outset to pay more of the bills and carry more of the financial load, but she grew to resent our arrangement. I would have paid more, but I couldn't afford it. Feeling guilty about my finances, I let things slide in the house that bothered me immensely, like coming home and finding other people had slept in my bed or discovering a big pile of dog shit on my floor. My room was up the stairs in the back of the house and didn't have a door, so I awoke often to kids playing at the bottom of the stairs. I think if I had been able to do more financially, things would have been a lot better.

This period was full of ups and downs. Elly and I went through a lot together and through it all I was rediscovering myself and figuring out who I was and who I wanted to be. At the same time, during that second year I got laid off, fell even more in debt, and was still struggling to finish school. On one very, very dark day I considered packing my bags and leaving. I thought my kids and family would be better off without me. Feeling like a failure doesn't begin to describe how I felt. I wasn't able to financially support myself, my kids, or get out of debt. The weight of all of this stifled my happiness and laughter and it seemed easier to change my identity and start over than it did to crawl out of the hole I had dug. I didn't understand why everything had to be so hard. It felt like I couldn't catch a break in any aspect of my life. My oldest son was around 15 and he decided I was a terrible mother. He chose to go live with his father for a while, ever verbal about my shortcomings. I didn't listen to him, I didn't care about him, I wanted to make him miserable. I was devastated. Somewhere inside I wondered if the awful things this teenager was saying were true. It felt like the walls were crashing in on me.

When I took stock of my life, all I saw was what I didn't have. I didn't have a husband. I didn't have a house of my own. I didn't have a job, a plan, or a degree. I did have a mountain of debt, two kids by two different dads, and a ton more classes needed to earn a degree. Looking back, it scares me how close I came that day to running. I seriously considered getting in my car and just driving to start anew somewhere else where no one knew anything about me. I went for a walk and found a bench overlooking the water. I had shunned God. I had questioned everything I had been taught, including His existence. I turned away from everything I believed in when I got divorced because God and divorce didn't seem to go together. I went to my room and wept. I wept like I hadn't in years, like I could feel the death of life as I had known it creeping from my skin and pooling on the floor. Out loud, through broken tears, I begged God for help and forgiveness. I had found my rock bottom and I wanted to get up. In that moment I spoke to Him just like I had spoken to my parents that awful day when I confirmed I was indeed pregnant. I hit my knees and prayed for help figuring out how to get out of the mess I unwillingly created.

I will never forget how quickly life turned around after that.

There is something about speaking out loud to the Universe, to God.

CHAPTER SIX

I'd questioned God before, of course. I think it's only human to do so. To question where we came from and why we are here is as old as time. I'd been a member of my church youth group for as long as I remembered and had gone through both communion and being confirmed in my Episcopal Church. I had attended church camp where I felt God's presence thoroughly as I sat by the fire singing with the other campers—a high I have only found again a few times. But none of my experiences with God, or the words from the church people that pushed him so, had ever prepared me for what would happen if I tried over and over again to do the right thing and still failed. I didn't know what came after rock bottom.

I didn't understand how Jesus taught love and acceptance but in reality, there were so many conditions placed on that acceptance, many of which I had already broken (or wanted to). Did I really deserve to rot in the depths of hell?

My new journey began that day on the floor. I like to think the tears that washed over me that day took a little piece of my self-doubt and replaced it with the courage to move forward. For the second time in my life, something else took over. I felt the same way now as I did as a teenage girl, the day I walked into the living room where my parents wept after they found out I was pregnant .Logically, I had nothing—no money, no ideas, and nowhere to go—but inside my life was changed. I was renewed. I was overcome with love and the knowledge that everything was going to be better than I could ever have imagined.

I was laid off from my job, I was broke, and had no idea what I was going to do. I was still working towards my bachelor's degree but I had over a year left to go. The living situation with Elly had deteriorated and I needed to get out and figure out what was next. With my new sense of hope, determination, and the realization that I could only go up from where I was, I decided what I wanted. I wanted to move back to the house that I owned, where the weeping willow tree stood in the front yard. I wanted to find a new job. I wanted to find someone to share my life with.

Instead of focusing on what I didn't have I decided to focus on what I did. I was still young, only 31, and I had my health. My kids were both healthy, too, and Hatteras adored me. Tyler was still angry at me and spent most of his time with his father but for the time being, it was a good thing for both of us. It allowed me to focus on school a little more and even though my relationship with his father and stepmother had been strained, I really needed their help and there were two of them to help tackle our teenager. I was thankful they lived close enough that we could work together and that while I was struggling, they were there for our son. By some miracle, not long after that day I wept on the floor, my tenants asked if they could get out of their lease early. I was thrilled. We were moving home.

My parents' friends had a daughter who needed a place to live, and so I let her move in with me and the boys. She had just finished school and was trying to get a job as a teacher. Her patience with my boys—and me—was just what I needed. I got a job working for a non-profit that paid more than I had ever made.

While my external world began shifting in more and more beneficial ways my internal world began to shift as well. I kept reading everything I could get my hands on to help figure out why I wasn't like everyone else and how exactly I could get on track. But then a funny thing happened. I found what I wasn't looking for. A realization so *shocking*, so inherently *unbelievable*, that it absolutely had to be true.

It was all bullshit.

Everything I had been taught was absolute crap. It was all made up. Everything I had been taught was just stories that had been passed down. I wasn't less than, or even alone, for having a baby as a teenager. I was still incredibly lovable and deserving of love. I realized that everyone believed what they had been taught and few ever questioned its validity. Elizabeth Gilbert had taken the world by storm with her book *Eat, Pray, Love* but it was her book *Committed* that changed my life. Marriage, to begin with, has a very sordid history in Christianity and isn't quite the pillar I had been led to believe. In fact, in most parts of the world, including ours, marriage is rarely just about love. It's a business decision, a way to manage wealth. It was created by male humans, not even Jesus or the big God upstairs. And, it didn't take a whole lot of research to discover that originally each man had multiple wives or to see that overall marriage has been shockingly unsuccessful at pairing one man with one woman for life.

The same year *Committed* was published, so was another book that would change my life: *Sex at Dawn: How we mate, why we stray, and what it means for modern relationships.*

While this book focuses on sex as it has evolved throughout human history, it ties in with the concept of marriage as it has changed as well. One of my favorite quotes from that book—found in the introduction and summing up what took me decades to comprehend— " The conflict between what we are *told* we feel and what we *really* feel may be the richest source of confusion, dissatisfaction, and unnecessary suffering of our time". Exactly. The book made me realize that I wasn't different, I was the same as everyone else. The rules I had been taught to follow were quite literally impossible to follow. The rules went against human nature. That living up to the standards that society had set, *that* was the impossibility. It wasn't that I had failed to be "good" or "normal," it was that I had made mistakes that were harder to hide than most people's.

To sum up some of what I learned through my journey of understanding relationships I found this to be the most profound: I unconditionally and overwhelmingly love both of my parents, both of my sisters, both of my sons, all of my friends—and yet, I am supposed to only love one romantic partner at a time? Or ever? It just didn't make sense.

When I was in high school and my early twenties I sincerely loved both Justin and Paul, and for different reasons. Paul was sincere and a hopeless romantic. Justin made me laugh and was the life of the party. I learned from those two relationships that I wanted someone with all of those qualities—and that had led me to Brad. Brad was exactly what I needed at 26, but he wasn't what I needed for the rest of my life—and that's okay. Ninety-five percent of the time he was the most amazing man I had ever dated, but the five percent of the time that he was awful ruined it all. I learned from him what I was willing to put up with and what I wasn't.

What would modern American life look like if we treated marriage like a wealth system and a family system but maybe not a sex system? Maybe marriage stories and love stories are two completely different things. Maybe monogamy is the single biggest and most destructive lie we've been sold. According to theories presented in *Sex at Dawn*, monogamy is the biggest enemy of the human race. By taking "survival of the fittest" out of reproduction we are systematically reducing sperm count. There are many studies to support the theory that the female vagina and other reproductive organs and processes are designed to actually take on sperm from multiple sources, and that sperm's entire function is to actually race other sperm. There are theories that say we are designed to raise our children within a village of people from the beginning, not behind a closed door where two adults try in isolation to become everything to each other and their children.

I saw it as a consequence of biology that my partner could cheat on me sexually and still love me completely. I wished I had known this sooner. I wish I had understood in high school that Justin could genuinely have had feelings for me, and for another girl, too. Love and sexual desire are not mutually exclusive. We do not need one to have the other and we can have them with the same people or completely separate people. It seemed to me that on some level, we all knew this. So why were we trying so hard not to acknowledge it? To say that the existence of these possibilities was wrong? Why did we pretend that the fiery depths of hell awaited any human who behaved in an innately human way?

As I learned, and continue to learn, I became aligned with who I was, less willing to pretend to be anything else. When I was married and I fell in love with someone else I could have simply lied and had an affair. I could have spent the rest of my life pushing down my overwhelming desire for Brad and wondering what could have been. I was hopelessly in love with him and the desire I had for him I had never had for another man, my husband included. While my husband had always made me feel less than, average, and just like every other woman he had been with sexually, Brad made me feel unique, special, and electric—long before we ever had sex. I can say with all honesty that hiding it and denying it was impossible.

What if from an evolutionary standpoint I was meant to marry and procreate with my husband because my son was destined to be on this Earth with our combined DNA, but once he arrived my journey with Justin was done? What if raising children together, sexual exclusivity, and marriage were the exception and not the norm? What if my children were actually better off being raised by a village (a mother and her husband, a father and his wife, and all of their extended family) than by just the two of us miserably chugging through life waiting to arrive at a headstone that shows my marriage *must* have been a success because it was long?

I was 26 years old, repulsed by a man that made me feel inferior, collapsed my sense of self, destroyed my self-esteem, and added absolutely zero to the "partnership" of our marriage. And yet, it was me that got shunned. It was me that "ruined" the marriage. It was me that "cheated" because I found solace in the arms of another, emotionally. It didn't matter at all that I was not in a sexual relationship—that I left before I did that because my conscience and moral code just wouldn't allow it. Everyone just assumed I was sleeping with Brad and I'll say it, my life would have been easier if I had. I benefited in no way by being honest with my husband and telling him I had feelings for someone else. The community as a whole didn't believe me anyway. Its been almost twenty years since I walked out of that door and Justin has spent the entire time convinced I had a sexual and sordid affair and has been very successful at allowing it to consume him. He can still barely speak to me. It doesn't matter how many girls he cheated on. It doesn't matter that our marriage was in shambles long before I got feelings for someone else. All that mattered was the story that got told, it didn't even matter if it was true.

The alternative of leaving my marriage was suicide. I wouldn't consider myself as having been "suicidal" but when I realized I would rather die than live another day with Justin, I knew it was time to go. How awful that we live in a society that encouraged me to stay. How different would my life, and Justin's —and our son's—have been if, when I went to him and told him that I was in love with Brad, he chose to talk to me? If he chose to believe that I was coming to him before I did something that I couldn't take back. If he could have acknowledged that we were both miserable and it was just time to call it? He told himself a story, and he made his life worse.

I had done the same. I had told myself a story that went like this:

I was just a girl, still young and dumb and naive, who ruined her life in 3 seconds by accidently getting pregnant. Because of this mistake no one of value would ever want to marry me or love me. I believed that because of my mistake I was inherently unlovable, that perhaps the only love I would ever have was from my son. My words were not worthy of respect and my thoughts and opinions were only good enough to be taken from me and used as comedy in the cafeteria. As a girl, with a baby, my only way out was to find a husband to support me. That happiness could only be found with a ring. That I should immediately have another child so that they would have each other to grow up with and because we were married it would all be okay. I believed that I was incapable of taking care of myself without the support of my father or my husband. That a road forged alone as a single parent was inherently *less* than a life lived in matrimony. Once you married, the second part of your life began.

But that story was wrong. I rewrote the story like this:

I was just a girl when a simple 3 seconds changed my life forever. I took responsibility for my actions and did what I thought was right at the time: I gave birth and kept my son. I was incredibly lucky that my family found a way to love me unconditionally and support me throughout what was a very difficult journey for all of us.

When I did find love and then marriage, I realized rather quickly that I had made a huge mistake. Instead of spending decades trying to figure it out, I left just shy of four years in and with a two-year-old on my hip. I found someone, rather unconventionally, that made me realize that I was lovable, that I was worthy, that my sexuality was defined by me, not by my husband. He saved my life. Even though he and I weren't written in the stars he was exactly what I needed right then. Because of my relationship with him I was able to realize what things were non-negotiable for me in a partnership. He made me see myself as an exceptional woman that defied convention, in a good way. I realized I was actually incredibly smart and capable of taking care of myself. That I was an exceptional person for thriving despite having a baby at sixteen. That my college degree could mean *more* because it was fought for not in the halls of a dorm but in the twilight hours before the world awoke while my children slept. That my life had built me, and created me, in a way that was unique to me, and I was better for it. I knew at twenty-six what some people didn't know until they were in their forties, if they ever knew. I fought, with everything in me, to become who I always wanted to be and I chose to learn from my mistakes and see them as speed bumps not roadblocks.

If I was going to tell myself a story, it was going to be a damn good one.

I was able to convince myself that having two kids already could be a good thing. There are actually men out there that are happy to be step-fathers but don't want their own children. There are men that can't have children. There are so many ways my story could unfold that I hadn't even thought of. No one else's story was any more "true" or "factual" than mine. I was on my own journey with my own lessons and challenges and I didn't need to live it like anyone else had. I decided to be thankful, proud even, of the character I had shown and the dedication I had exhibited to living my truth. I had to come to terms that it didn't matter what anyone else believed about my story, it only mattered what I knew and believed.

And somewhere in there the "poor me" turned in to WATCH ME.

Watch me as I glide across this stage to get my Bachelor's degree at 33.

Watch me as I become an Entrepreneur with multiple businesses.

Watch me as I blossom into the writer I always dreamed I would be.

Watch me turn 27 years of single parenting into a career where I am an expert on co-parenting.

Watch me become a real estate investor.

Watch me get my Masters degree.

Watch me go from that pregnant little girl to a successful woman.

Watch me.

CHAPTER SEVEN

The year was 2017 and I was just shy of 39. It was late June and we had transitioned from spring into a beautiful summer. For the past eight months I had been working for my father's construction company. I woke up early each day and dressed in jeans and a bright yellow shirt, then drove into the office for a 5 a.m. start time. Once there, I would gather what I would need for the day—steel-toe boots, hard hat—and then head into the shipyard.

I was the Superintendent for a huge project that involved managing workers and sub-contractors, performing quality assurance on our work, and meeting stringent deadlines.

The building we were working on was enormous and was being built beside the James River. Despite the chaos of the daily grind, the river brought me peace each day. I was on-site most of the day and had a trailer to work in as needed. The job was constantly behind, and we had sub-contractors working almost around the clock to catch up. There was a lot of pressure on me to get it right from external sources but the internal voice is what plagued me.

I can hear my father telling me fifteen years earlier that he would never employ me at his company because it was "no place for a girl" and I can feel his eyes on me wondering if he has made a huge mistake, looking over my work and anxious for updates from the field. If he hasn't made a huge mistake by hiring me, and I am successful, I know he will swell with pride at his legacy. If I fail, the stakes are too high to fathom. What I didn't know on that particular day is how little any of it mattered.

In April, in the middle of our big project at work, my parents sat me and my youngest sister down for a family meeting. Sitting on my parents back deck around a fire pit my dad announced that he had been diagnosed with stage IV Lung Cancer. This was my worst fear—and one I had been mentally preparing for, for more than thirty years. His father, the one who introduced me first to grief when I was only 10, died at 63 of lung cancer and since my dad had been a heavy smoker up until two years before, I always knew this fate was a real possibility. He would be 64 on June 4.

But on that spring day those thoughts were far from my mind. My body took to shaking, as if I was freezing, and didn't stop. My father, who must have rehearsed this speech many times before our arrival, told us that he had lived an incredible life and that he didn't know why he had been so lucky. He said that he had done and seen so much more than he would have ever thought was possible. His speech continued but after that I don't remember a word. I was trying so desperately to stop the tears from coming and I just couldn't anymore. I looked at my sister and asked her to drive me home.

My father and I had been through a lot. This was the man who helped me paint the mailbox as a girl, who took me to submarine launches at the shipyard and taught me not to be afraid of snakes. He was the same man who had asked me, when he found out that I was pregnant, if I "even knew who the father was." He was the same man I managed to completely ignore for almost two years as a teenager. But in the intervening years, he had become someone different. I had become someone different, too. Somewhere along the line he had become my greatest confidant, someone I spent most of my free time with, and, recently, my boss. Our relationship had transformed and blossomed. He was the first person I would turn to when life threw me things that I didn't know how to handle. The two of us together could sit and talk for hours and would almost always end up laughing until we cried. We shared a passion for boating, spending time with our friends, enjoying the little things—like time with each other or our friends—and building things. We once almost started a company that sold a "wine weight" which could be inserted into a box of wine in order to push the wine out once the bag got to the bottom. The year before he had helped me start a new business flipping houses. We had carefully selected the house and he was with me every step of the way as I renovated and then sold the house for a profit. Even though I worked for him, he had introduced me to someone he knew as a writer, one of the single most important moments of my life.

I had been watching my father dwindle away, watched him deal with the ramifications of both chemo and radiation, for about six weeks or so when my mother and I took him to an appointment at Duke University, where he hoped the doctors might give him a more optimistic diagnosis than he had gotten from the local hospital. When we arrived, my father, once a muscular man who had worked with his hands for over forty years, stepped on the scale to reveal that he and I weighed almost the same thing. The diagnosis from the doctors at Duke was not promising.

In an attempt to spend every second with him, I moved back in with my parents. I stayed in the small apartment above their detached garage, overlooking Jones Creek.

One Saturday, I woke up and headed out the door around 5 a.m., just like always, for a full day of work. As I descended the stairs into the workshop area for my departure I turned the corner and screamed. My father was sitting in a chair. He hadn't left his bed in weeks—he scared me half to death! Once my heart began to calm, I chatted with him for a second. I was so happy to see him up and able to talk. I wished I could spend the whole day there beside him, talking. Instead, I hugged him and went to work with a shirt bearing the logo of his company.

When things got progressively worse and the hospice nurse informed us that we had only a few days left, I stopped going to work—even though I know that would have angered him. But I got up early each morning and relieved the night nurse. I sat with him and talked to him, even though he could not respond. He lay in his hospital bed a small sliver of the man he was just a few months ago. I held his hand and tried to memorize the lines in them and the way they felt. His hands were much smaller than they used to be, but they were still as warm and comforting as they were when I was 15, the night he sat on my bed and held my hand and told me he didn't want my pregnancy to stop me from becoming the person I wanted to be. I couldn't imagine never holding his hand again.

I told him how much I loved him and that I couldn't watch him go. That I just didn't have it in me to watch the greatest man I had ever known leave this Earth. And so, when I left to go see my therapist, he passed away peacefully, just moments after I left the driveway.

He waited for me to leave and honored my wish. Even in his last moments he figured out how to give me a gift.

I lived with my parents for just two weeks. In that time, I was able to have a few special moments I know I wouldn't have gotten otherwise. We didn't get to have any end-of-life goodbyes because by the time I realized he really wasn't going to make it, it was too late. I wonder if that's how it happened for him, too.

Nothing could have prepared me for how death changed me.

My grief was overwhelming, so much so that I went completely numb for months. I was incapable of feeling anything except sadness and grief. I am sure that my family needed me but I didn't notice. I am sure there was laughter but I just couldn't feel it. Sleep never came. Love lost its meaning.

On top of our grief, my family now had a very difficult decision to make. We had to decide what to do with my father's company. Despite his best efforts, we hadn't had enough time together to figure it all out before his death. As an employee, and his daughter, I had a conflict of interest and needed to decide if I was going to stay or go. On the one hand, I knew how proud my father had been to have me working at his company. Arriving each day at work I could feel his comforting presence as I entered his office and saw his name on everything. On the other hand, the reminders of him were painful and everywhere. Every time I saw a document with his name on it, my heart grew heavy. In the end I realized that I had enjoyed working there but it was he who made me enjoy it. Without him it was just work, and not my soul's work. I remembered him introducing me as a writer. He knew I would find my happiness not between the four walls of a construction trailer, but between the pages of a book. I decided to leave the company and we decided to sell it to the top three employees.

That decision and subsequent sale took us through another year, during which I tried to find what it was that fed my soul and how exactly I could build a life that supported it. I had remarried five years earlier and my husband was supportive of me trying to find what would make me happy but he had no more answers than I did. Ultimately,

I decided to get my real estate license and focus on my real estate investment company full-time. I had learned so much from the one flip I had done with my dad that I was able to feel confident doing it on my own.

Recently, I used my father's signature to have my maiden name tattooed on my forearm.

It's a simple reminder to me of both my father and who I am at my core. A reminder that I am his daughter and nothing can change that. That I want to build the life he knew I could and make him proud. While I believe I have done that, I still venture on.

The story doesn't end until I do.

The good news is that from here on out, I get to write the story. I get to create and recreate it whenever I want. I have recreated my life from scratch at least twice now. I can't help but be proud of myself for the things I have overcome and the ways my life has changed in such unexpected ways. I'm also struck by how my journey sculpted and changed the views and life of others, such as my parents. That couple from the 80s was forced to change their view of what it was like to have daughters, of what women are capable of, and what the sentence should be for a girl who gets pregnant at sixteen.

I know I am not the only successful "recovered" teen mom but sometimes it sure feels like I am. It's the last piece of information I like to share with people and the look in their eyes confirms that it's pretty shocking. And I like that. I like that no stereotype can define me. That my life story really doesn't make sense at all. That I have been rich and poor, that I barely graduated from high school but now I am working on my PhD. Without all the bullshit, the mistakes, and the drama, I wouldn't have a story to tell at all. And that's the point of it all, I think. The traditional nuclear family I grew up in was amazing, but so was the tapestry family I gave my kids. Marrying and creating a family together is beautiful, but is just one way of doing life. I find comfort, acceptance, and peace in not being any of things I was "supposed to" or expected to be. The further away from the status quo, the happier I became.

The thing I wanted most of all my entire life, from childhood on, was acceptance and an embracing of me from me. I discovered that when I gave myself the freedom to be me, I also found it from others. There is beauty in originality. There is no normal. We are all original and we are all writing our own stories—or we could be.

ABOUT THE AUTHOR

L eslie is a Doctoral student studying perspectives of joint shared custody through the eyes of adults who have aged out of the two-home system. She holds a B.S. in Psychology from Old Dominion University and a Master of Public Administration from Walden University. She is also a CDC Certified Divorce Coach, CDC Transition and Recovery Coach, member of ICF, real estate investor & agent, author, wife, and mother of two adult sons. They reside in Suffolk, VA.

In addition to her educational experience, Leslie also survived teen pregnancy in 1994, a divorce in 2005, and the death of her father in 2017. Each of these experiences brought change that she learned to embrace, including co-parenting both in and out of the 50/50 joint shared custody arena for 27 years. Her teen pregnancy and subsequent parenting took her through mediation, parenting classes, multiple court cases, child support, and all types of custody arrangements. Her divorce was a life-changing occurrence that took her from the life she thought she always wanted to a completely new life she had never even dared to dream of. Her experiences turning a life destined for failure into a life of abundance have inspired her to help others embrace hope & happiness—and make it through divorce better than you were.